THOMAS GRAY'S JOURNAL

of his Visit to the Lake District in October 1769

Edited
with a Life, Commentary, and Historical Background
by

WILLIAM ROBERTS

Liverpool University Press

2001

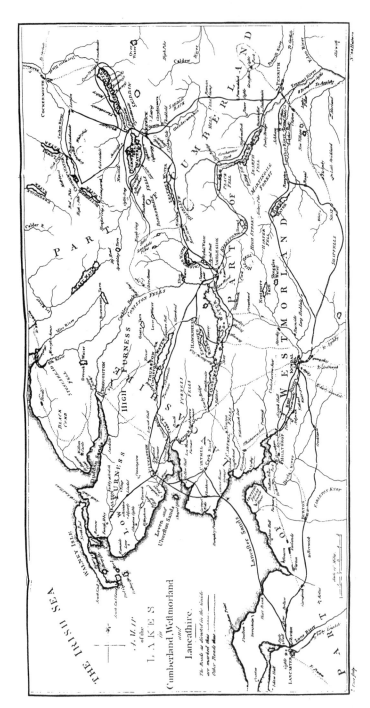

The Lake District, from Thomas West's *Guide to the Lakes*, 1780

TO ANNE

Two poets:
one of skied, and inward personal, ode,
and elegy - lyrist of arrowy stress,
the filtered phrase: the other unacknowledged
poet of field and wood, flower, temperatures
and weathers; whose eye incised appearance
and behaviour with ageless, lucid
words. Another man who used
to notice such things.

From *For Thomas Gray* by Alastair Macdonald

First published 2001 by
Liverpool University Press
4 Cambridge Street
Liverpool L69 7ZU

British Library Cataloguing-in-Publication data
A British Library CIP record is available

ISBN 0-85323-667-4

Printed and bound in the European Union by Bookcraft Ltd, Midsomer
Norton, Wilts

CONTENTS

ILLUSTRATIONS

PREFACE

THE main object of this book is to make the text of Gray's *Journal* of his tour in the Lake District more widely available. However, it also seeks, in the introduction, to set that journal in the context of Gray's life and personality and, in the conclusion, to place it in the context of the growing awareness of wild nature that took place at the end of the eighteenth century. The "tailpieces" try to make something useful of the inevitable typographical gaps by finding a place for snippets of Gray's *obiter dicta*, from notebooks and marginalia, which perhaps reveal a little more of the man. The journal itself brings together a number of activities, reading, thinking, experience, and the commentary therefore aims, not merely to footnote the text with explanations, but more widely to engage with issues about how we appreciate and conserve wild scenery, challenged by the thinking and experience of a former age. There is an underlying anxiety, in my part of the book, that we have lost the awe and the magic that Gray found, and a belief (that is part hope) that it is still there to be retrieved, if you know where and when to look.

TEXTUAL NOTE

THERE are two authorial texts for the journal, neither complete. The earlier is the two notebooks in the possession of Mr John Murray, which appear to be the original manuscript as written by Gray, in notebooks already in use for other miscellaneous material, during his journey in October 1769. These have a number of corrections but are neat and fluent, in Gray's characteristic careful handwriting. They look almost too neat to have been written up day by day. Unfortunately, a considerable portion of the text is missing: the first notebook begins with the words, " the largest not 8 feet high" in the middle of the entry for 5th October. Presumably there must have been an earlier notebook but there is no indication in any bibliographical record of what happened to it.

The other text is given in four letters to Thomas Wharton in the British Library (Egerton MS 2400) and edited by Toynbee and Whibley in their collection of Gray's correspondence in 1935. Gray copied out his journal, after his return, into letters for the benefit of his friend, Dr Thomas Wharton, who had been unable to accompany him on his journey. The first letter was sent from Aston (Mason's home) on 18th October on his way to Cambridge, with the first two days of the journal. Gray sent a further instalment of 3½ days from Cambridge on 29th October, and a third from Cambridge in November. Not until January did he send the instalment for 5th to 8th October, and the last section was not sent at all, only existing (in the Egerton MS) in a transcript. The letters have the further slight complication that they also contain postscripts and additional material, not only written after Gray's visit but not relevant to it, which need to be omitted from a journal version.

Neither text, therefore, is completely satisfactory in itself. The only solution is a combined text, using the letters up to the point at which the Murray notebooks begin and then giving preference to the Murray notebooks text. Toynbee and Whibley also used a combined text but they gave the preference to the text in the letters to a further point (in the middle of the entry for 9th October) and only used the Murray notebooks for the transcribed letter, which began at that point. Their aim was to give the most authentic text for the letters. My aim is to give the most authentic text for the journal and there is no doubt that the Murray notebooks are nearer to Gray's original intentions. I have also set the text out as a journal, because this is how it originally was, rather than as letters, omitting non-journal material. Some additional material from the Egerton MS is given in square brackets, and also in square brackets, where it seems helpful, I have included modern spellings alongside Gray's old or mis-spelt originals. Readers may like to be warned that Gray did not usually capitalize the beginnings of sentences and used a number of abbreviations in superscript, such as wch for "which".

A NOTE ON JOSEPH FARINGTON

Joseph Farington was born at Leigh in Lancashire in 1747, the son of a clergyman. He became a pupil of the artist, Richard Wilson, and was elected to the Royal Academy in 1785. He made two collections of engraved views of the Lake District, one published in 1789 and the other in 1816. He is known to have been an admirer of Gray and timed his first visit to Keswick in 1775 to coincide with the month chosen by Gray (October). It was William Gilpin's view that it was not necessary for anyone else to draw the Lake District accurately "because Mr Farington had already done that". He died as the result of a fall in 1821.

Overleaf: Thomas Gray, by J. G. Eckhardt

INTRODUCTION

The Life and Personality of Thomas Gray

THE drawing room of John Murray's, the publishers, is an elegant eighteenth-century room, high-ceilinged and book-lined, hung with the portraits of the distinguished authors who have met there. To handle the original manuscript of a great writer anywhere is an exciting experience; to open Gray's *Journal* in this room, almost under the gaze of his portrait (in the next room), was more than an exceptional privilege. It was to move back two centuries and more towards the moment when it was written and into the presence of the writer. To read that neat, regular handwriting in those surroundings was quickly to come into the company of a warm-hearted, good-humoured man, mentally robust, highly intelligent, sensitive to place and to people - a thoroughly likeable and pleasant man, with whom it would have been a pleasure to walk through the Lake District. One's first reaction was to be certain that this book must be published. Next, one wanted to know more about the author, to have some outline of his life, and then to have some explanation of his character. What follows is an attempt at such a background. The outline is not complex, though, as with most eighteenth-century lives, there are a number of indistinct areas and some unanswered questions.

Gray's Birth and Childhood

Thomas Gray was born in Cornhill in London on 26th December, 1716, the fifth child of Philip Gray, a scrivener, and of Dorothy Gray, née Antrobus. According to the standard biographies, Dorothy had eleven children but the others all died at various stages of childhood, Thomas being the only survivor. According to the parish registers for St Michael's, Cornhill, however, Dorothy had only ten children, of two of whom there is no further record, presumed died young. Of the other eight, two (besides Thomas) in fact survived beyond a few months. A first Philip lived to the age of three years and a second Philip lived a similar span. The father, Philip Gray, had previously been married and had had two children by that marriage. Both these children and, of course, the wife had died. These details are worth elaborating because they make clear the appalling surroundings of repeated births, sicknesses and early deaths by which Thomas's childhood was surrounded and the guilt which he may have felt as the only survivor, or at least the insecurity and fear. This fact, of which the standard biographies make little, is surely crucial. At one crisis of health in his childhood Gray apparently suffered a fit, from which he was allegedly only saved by his mother's opening a vein with her scissors, "by that means relieving the determination of the blood to the brain" (according to the nineteenth-century biographer, Edmund Gosse). In fact, though blood-letting was an accepted practice at the time, Mrs Gray may well have done more harm than good. It is more than ever a miracle that Thomas survived, his febrile convulsions perhaps indicating some inherited weakness. We also know that Gray's father was violent and abusive towards his wife. By 1735, after 25 years of marriage, the situation was so bad that Gray's mother applied to a Dr John Audley for legal advice on the possibility of taking action in the courts against her husband. The complaint was that "almost ever since he hath been married, he hath used her in the most inhuman manner, by beating, kicking, punching, and with the most vile and abusive language". What Dorothy Gray appeared also to be afraid of was that her husband had the long-term intention of driving her out of her business with her sister as a milliner. It would appear that she relied on this business to finance Thomas at school and that she received no financial support from her husband. The law at that time was of no help to her, since Dr Audley reported back that the most the courts would be prepared to tolerate was a separation and that this would be only in extreme circumstances. How extreme did they have to be, one wonders? Thomas's childhood must therefore have been unhappy, violent, insecure, made tolerable only by the love of his mother, for whom he not surprisingly developed a strong and close affection, and by the care of his mother's brothers, Thomas and Robert Antrobus. It is hard to think of a major writer with a less promising childhood.

Eton College and Cambridge

At the age of eleven he was sent to school at Eton College, at his mother's expense. One might have thought that the apparently slight, quiet Gray would have had a hard time of it but the reverse was true: he thrived. Perhaps as an *oppidan* (a lodger in the town) he experienced a less strict discipline; perhaps he was lucky in his boarding house. The life of a colleger was proverbially strict and harsh and Gray recommended to his friend, Wharton, in a letter in 1761, that he sent his son to Eton as an *oppidan*, so that he might avoid "the hardships of College". The teaching, at least in the classics, must have been excellent, and he lived in a protected world of congenial friends. There may well be an element of idealization in Gray's re-creation of that "careless childhood" in the *Eton College* ode but he clearly looked back on those days as a time of happy innocence, swimming, playing trap-ball, walking along the river-banks, clearly not taking part in the rougher traditions of those times, such as hunting the ram. He became a member of a close-knit, supportive group of four friends, the other three being Richard West, Thomas Ashton, and Horace Walpole. Gray's friendship with the Keats-like figure of West was particularly close and passionate, though his friendship with Walpole, the son of the Prime Minister, was more important to him socially and in his later literary life. Gray went up to Cambridge as a pensioner (one who pays his own expenses) at Peterhouse in 1734, Walpole following (to King's) in 1735. However, Gray left Cambridge in 1738 without taking a degree, for reasons about which we can only speculate: he may have disliked the mathematical content of the syllabus; he may have decided that, since the only point of a degree would be to qualify him for a career in the church - which clearly did not appeal - he would be better to begin qualifying for a legal career instead. Gray's problem was, in the absence of independent means, to find a career which would give him a livelihood and leave him free to pursue at least some of the pleasures of a cultured life. At all events he left Cambridge in September 1738, retreating to his father's house in London for six months, until a providential event changed the course of his life.

The Grand Tour with Horace Walpole

In the spring of 1739 Horace Walpole needed a companion to accompany him on his Grand Tour. He asked Gray to join him, undertaking to pay all Gray's expenses. It was a generous offer, even if the subordinate relationship to a man of Walpole's rank, position, and mercurial temperament was a dangerous one. The two friends left Dover at the end of March 1739 and travelled via Amiens to Paris. They stayed in Paris for two months and then moved on to Rheims. In September they moved to the south of France and then travelled through the Haute Savoie to Geneva. From Geneva they returned to Lyons, from there crossing the Alps into Italy. In Italy they spent some time in Genoa and Florence and by March 1740 they were in Rome. After a few weeks they returned to Florence, staying there for the following winter. In April 1741 they were in Reggio (between Parma and Modena), where a quarrel occurred, as a result of which Gray parted from Walpole and returned by a circuitous route to England.

There were a number of highlights to this tour. One was an evening's entertainment at Rheims, which Gray described in a letter to his mother. It is worth quoting at some length since its picture of Gray socializing into the small hours of the morning is different from what we might expect from the standard assumptions about his quiet and retiring nature.

It is sure they do not hate gaity any more than the rest of their country-people, and can enter into diversions, that are once proposed, with a good grace enough: for instance, the other evening we happened to be got together in a company of eighteen people, men and women of the best fashion here, at a garden in the town to walk; when one of the ladies bethought herself of asking, Why should we not sup here? Immediately the cloth was laid by the side of a fountain under the trees, and a very elegant supper served up; after which another said, Come let us sing; and directly began herself: From singing we insensibly fell to dancing, and singing in a round; when somebody mentioned the violins, and immediately a company of them was ordered: Minuets were begun in the open air, and then came country dances, which held till four o'clock next morning; at which hour the gayest lady proposed, that such as were weary should get into their coaches, and the rest of them should dance before them with the music in the van; and in this manner we paraded through all the principal streets in the city, and waked everybody in it. [21 June 1739]

Another significant event was his visit to the monastery of the Grande Chartreuse. This is remotely situated in the Dauphiné Alps and the journey there through the mountains deeply impressed Gray and moved him by its beauty, silence, and dangers. "In our little journey up to the Grande Chartreuse, I do not remember to have gone ten paces without an exclamation that there was no restraining: Not a precipice, not a torrent, not a cliff, but is pregnant with religion and poetry. There are certain scenes that would awe an atheist into belief without the help of other argument" [16 Nov. 1739]. He made a point of returning there on his way home two years later and composed a Latin ode for the visitor's book of the monastery. It is a fine poem either in Latin, if you have enough of the language to respond to it, or in English, as it is translated at the end of this book as an epilogue. It gives expression to the religious experience of finding some spiritual presence in the mountains and to the desire for peace and silence. In the eighteenth century Latin verse was sometimes used to give vent to more personal feeling than would be thought appropriate to the formal verse of the day. Crossing the Alps by the Mont Cenis pass later in the year repeated the impression that mountain scenery made upon him. "Mont Cenis," he confessed in a letter to West, "carries the permission mountains have of being frightful rather too far; and its horrors were accompanied with too much danger to give one time to reflect upon their beauties" [16 Nov. 1739]. During the crossing, poor Walpole had lost his pet black spaniel, ironically named Tory, seized and devoured by a wolf!

Gray also spent a good deal of his time on the tour looking at paintings, visiting great buildings, going to concerts, and in making notes that show his developing and independent tastes. He made a collection of manuscript music for 222 arias, duets and songs and notes on over 250 paintings in Italy, commenting on most of them individually. As the critic Jean Hagstrum observes, "His knowledge and judgement in the fine arts went far beyond that of the average poet-traveller of even the antiquarian eighteenth century".

What caused the quarrel between Gray and Walpole is unknown, any clues being hidden by Mason's censoring of the letters and by Gray's own reticence. The most likely cause is the one given in later years by Walpole, that the quarrel arose from the social difference between the two men and from Walpole's tactless aggravation of Gray's sensibilities in this regard. Other, more sensational interpretations are possible. It may be that Walpole made some homosexual advance, which Gray repelled: the issue of homosexuality is considered later in this chapter. Such an event would explain the reticence: it would not explain the *rapprochement* some years later.

Death of Gray's Father and of Richard West

Gray returned to a number of problems. The basic problem of obtaining a livelihood was aggravated by the extravagance of his father, who had managed to squander the family fortune before dying in November 1741. His mother, however, disposed of her business and was able to live on the assets, setting up house at Stoke Poges in Buckinghamshire. She was also able presumably to finance Gray in preparing for a career in the law. His friend West also intended to become a lawyer but died, probably of consumption, in March 1742. West's death affected Gray deeply. His poetic career appears to arise from the regret that he felt for the loss of his closest friend. His sonnet on West's death is a moving poem in itself but the *Elegy Written in a Country Churchyard* also seems to have arisen, like Milton's *Lycidas*, from the shock of early death. Gray's poetic career is remarkably short but some of his best poems belong to this first phase in the 1740s: *Ode to Spring, Ode on a Distant Prospect of Eton College, Ode on Adversity* and the *Elegy* itself.

The Remainder of his Life at Cambridge and in London

Gray's response to the problem of livelihood was to become a fellow-commoner at Peterhouse at Cambridge. This gave him a roof over his head and leisure in which to study and write, but on a condition: that he remained celibate. Enforced celibacy of this kind was not uncommon in the eighteenth century and there were strategies for coming to terms with it. It was a commonplace in London, according to Corbyn Morris in 1751, that "the unmarried Ladies and Gentlemen in this City, of moderate Fortunes, are unable to support the expense of a Family, with any Magnificence [....] they, therefore, acquiesce in Celibacy; Each Sex compensating itself, as it can, by other Diversions". The twentieth century tends to assume that all men possess an equally powerful sex drive but there are some whose sexual energy is low and who seem to be able to accept celibacy. It may warp them somewhat, they may need travel or escapist literature to divert them, they may occasionally be prone to depression, they may adopt other safety valves such as prostitution or pornography. We do not know by what route Gray survived. He claimed that the answer was to keep himself busy: "The receipt [for happiness] is obvious, Have something to do" [Letter to Walpole, 11 July 1757]. At all events the sexual problem does not seem to have been the major problem of his life.

Part of the answer and part of the problem was that the rest of Gray's life was, in a sense, the life of a hermit. He had some friends, of course, and many interests and activities, but the structure of his life was such as to emphasize his inwardness and isolation: it must have been, for much of the time, a dreary existence, which he appears not to have had the courage to break out of. In 1745 he resumed his friendship with Walpole, if not on terms of the same warmth, at least in ways that were useful to his literary career: it was Walpole who first circulated the *Elegy* and organized the publication of six of his poems with illustrations by Richard Bentley. Gray also developed other friendships in the 40s: with William Mason, Thomas Wharton, and Henrietta Speed. Mason was a bad poet and not very sensible into the bargain but he had his uses as an admirer; Thomas Wharton on the other hand appears to have been eminently sensible and pleasant and to have brought the best out of Gray; Henrietta Speed seems to have possessed everything that would have made her a good wife - high spirits and a fortune - but Gray missed his chance for reasons that are not clear. In 1753 Gray's mother died. She had been the making and preservation of him and he was devoted to her: when his own time came he was buried with her in the Antrobus family grave at Stoke Poges.

Gray had short spells of living in London, where he worked in the newly opened British Museum on esoteric research projects for his own personal pleasure. In 1756 he moved from Peterhouse across the road to Pembroke, allegedly as a result of an undergraduate practical joke: he is supposed to have been morbidly fearful of fire and to have been frightened by a false alarm. This patronizing assumption of Gray's timorousness appears to have little basis in fact. If Gray was afraid of fire, perhaps he was wise to be so in an age when fires were both more possible and more difficult to deal with.

Gray's financial worries eased as his life progressed and he gradually acquired a degree of affluence, particularly after he was appointed Professor of Modern History at Cambridge in 1768, with a stipend of £400 a year. He can be criticized for not lecturing and for treating the post as a sinecure but he undoubtedly began by planning to give lectures and to fulfil what were now being suggested to be the teaching duties of the post. Even before this more comfortable income, he began to indulge himself with annual tours. Although he never repeated anything on the scale of his Grand Tour, he did spend some time in most years in journeying round the country, to friends' houses, to beauty spots like the River Wye, and of course to London periodically. In 1764 he had set out on what he called his "Lilliputian travels", a tour of the south coast based on Southampton. In 1765 he did a five-day tour of the Highlands of Scotland. In 1766 he holiday-ed for a couple of months in Kent. In 1767 he made a first attempt at visiting the Lakes, cut short by the illness of Dr Wharton. His letters are the main record of these journeys but there are also some small note-books with short entries about the weather or flowers, trees or birds.

Gray's Death

His death came suddenly and relatively early at the age of 54 in July 1771. It is not clear why he died but the sudden sickness sounds like a perforated ulcer or peritonitis; Gosse called it "gout". Whatever the cause was, it was not over-drinking on the one hand or congenital heart disease on the other. Nor does Gray, despite traditions to the contrary, appear to have been a constitutional invalid, though he certainly had spells of depression. He could and should have lived longer.

A Survey of Gray's Character

As one looks back over this life, some salient features appear: his loneliness and isolation; his need to travel; his delicacy; his sexuality; his warmth and sociability; his sense of humour; his learning; his varied interests in painting, heraldry, botany, ornithology, cooking, and genealogy; and also some of his religious and political beliefs and his moral standards of personal behaviour.

His Isolation

The outstanding feature of Gray's personality is his isolation. He walks on his own for most of the time. He thinks to himself; he writes for himself. He is totally alone, in the bedroom at night and on the footpath by day. Apart from the years of the Grand Tour with Walpole, he rarely lived a shared life. Yet he pined for friendship. No wonder at times he sank into depression. "Mine you know," he confessed in a letter to West, "is a white melancholy" [27 May 1742].

His Need to Travel

Gray's temperament and his course of life was such that he needed a regular dose of travel therapy. This restlessness may well have been a consequence of Gray's loneliness or of some unfilled void. His diurnal existence, his norm, was excessively self-contained and self-occupying: reading and studying and occasionally writing. He needed to break that routine from time to time with long journeys. "Travel I must, or cease to be," he wrote in one of his last letters to Wharton [24 May 1771]. "I owe my late & present ease to the little expeditions I always make in summer," he wrote at much the same time to Walpole [17 Sept. 1770].

His Delicacy

There seems little point in pretending that Gray was not a delicate man, delicate in physique, delicate in aesthetic tastes, delicate in social sensibilities. There is plenty of evidence of this delicacy, including an accusation of "effeminacy" by the Revd William Temple, a contemporary of Gray's at Cambridge, and his own admission of fussiness at several times. There is, however, some point in objecting to the exaggeration of this fussiness into old-maid-ism. He did not become disagreeably maudlin but remained robust in his opinions and actions. Matthew Arnold attempted to deal with the problem a century ago. "His reserve, his delicacy, his distaste for many of the persons and things surrounding him in the Cambridge of that day [....] have produced an impression of Gray as being a man falsely fastidious, finical, effeminate." Gray also has a false reputation for being over-fussy about his health. David Cecil says that he watched his health as a scientist watches an experiment but there is very little evidence for this, none at all in the *Journal*. Gray certainly did badger his doctor-friend Wharton for help and advice on the workings of his bowels, which he treated, curiously and uncomfortably, with soap, but the eighteenth century was obsessed with self-medication, as a look at the adverts of any newspaper of the time will show, and I suspect that most people with medical friends consult them privately. Gray was no different from thousands of others, then or now, one might add. He had a surgical operation for the removal of piles, which he mockingly exaggerates and quickly recovered from but which his biographer Gosse treats as life-threatening. He complained from time to time of some minor gout or rheumatism in his legs. What he did suffer from, as has been mentioned, was a periodically returning depression, a white melancholy or the hyp, as he variously calls it, a morbid depression of spirits sufficiently numbing to bring him to a stop. His pocket book for 1755 has long gaps followed by notes in Latin: "pectoris oppressio & dolor"; "nox inquieta"; "nox turbida capitis". This is not physical illness that he is watching and lying awake with.

His Sexuality

Gray's sexuality is hardly relevant to his visit to the Lakes but, because it is currently a major biographical problem, it seems best to present some of the arguments. It is certainly assumed in many academic circles that Gray was homosexual, the main evidence being Gray's devotion to his school friend, Richard West, and his later passionate affection for the young Victor de Bonstetten, as revealed in his letters to him. Ketton-Cremer judged that Gray "found himself more and more obsessed with this handsome youth, and feeling an affection that alarmed him". Ketton-Cremer clearly implied more and later critics have been less inhibited in their speculations. They may be right, of course, but the pieces of evidence are insubstantial. Gray's passionate friendships with West and Bonstetten, common enough in a sexually divided society, are homosocial certainly but not physically homosexual in any sense that we now recognize. Not only does it not help to think of Gray as struggling with unrealized or unpermitted homosexuality, it can lead us astray. If there is an explanation available to us now, it may be that we should think of him as imprisoned by the psychological aftermath of a traumatic childhood. In his *Souvenirs*, written in 1831, Bonstetten describes the emotional vacuum he found in Gray. *Je crois que Gray n'avait jamais aimé, c'était le mot de l'enigme, il en était resulté une misère de coeur, qui faisait contraste avec son imagination ardente et profonde qui au lieu de faire le bonheur de sa vie, n'en était que le torment. Gray avait de la gaieté dans l'esprit et de la mélancholie dans la charactère.*[1] Bonstetten sounds a little pretentious but he was an intelligent man and his words pick out key features of Gray's temperament.

His Sociability

Gray was not unsociable. His letters show a range of different correspondents, together with a change in Gray himself to accommodate each one. To his friend William Mason he could be coarse and tactlessly rude. To Horace Walpole, the friend of his early years, he could be lively and skittish. To West and Bonstetten he could be passionately loving. To Wharton, however, the recipient of this journal, he is level-headed, good-humoured, sympathetic and trusting.

---

1. "I believe that Gray had never loved: that was the explanation of the enigma. It resulted in a misery in his heart which contrasted with his ardent and profound imagination, which, instead of making a happiness of his life, was only a torment. Gray had gaiety in his spirit and melancholy in his character."

Wharton seems to bring out the best in him, to be someone with whom he felt he could be fully and naturally himself. He clearly enjoyed Wharton's manly company, shared his interests, enjoyed the friendship of his wife, the love of his daughters, and the comfort of his home. He also seems to have mixed easily with his social inferiors, with a farmer in Borrowdale and with working people whom he met at inns on the way. The reverse was not true: he was very uneasy with social superiors and constantly aware of his comparatively lowly origins. He never quite managed to deal with the fame which he acquired after the publication of the *Elegy*. He remained a very shy man with strangers. The thought of having his portrait published as a frontispiece to some of his poems moved him to real distress.

His Sense of Humour

Gray's sense of humour, by way of contrast, is strong. It is self-deprecating, at times whimsical, usually kindly to those in his inner circle but sometimes cutting and sarcastic to others. It is the most important feature of anyone's character to those on the receiving end, because it is the essential connector to the real world and the social lubricant that makes all things bearable. One example of that sense of humour at work is in his description in the journal of the goats at Gordale Scar: "one of them danced and scratched an ear with its hind foot in a place where I would not have stood stockstill for all beneath the moon". The picture of the insouciant goat is itself funny but Gray uses it to mock his own caution, implicitly admitted and criticized, and gives it a pretty literary flavour with his quotation from Edgar's description of Dover Cliff in *King Lear*. One would happily walk with a man as warm-hearted as this, even if he did express a preference for safe paths.

His Learning

Gray had the reputation of being one of the most learned men in Europe, a reputation verifiable by a look at the list of the contents of his personal library. It is crushingly heavy: full of the Greek and

Latin classics, grammars and dictionaries, histories and biographies, the great poets and playwrights, literature in French, Italian, German, Icelandic and Welsh. One also needs to look at the nature of the books within that list, William Dugdale's *Baronage of England*, for example, two huge volumes packed with small print on the great aristocratic families, with no visible system of arrangement and no concessions to easy reading. Of this learning, however, nothing came by way of book or lecture, only the painstaking notes in neat, small writing for his own consumption in the common-place books at Cambridge or in the margins of his own books, now scattered across learned libraries all over the English-speaking world. Of the sharpness and complexity of that mind there is, however, no doubt.

His Beliefs

His beliefs seem to have been strong but conventional: Whiggish in politics, conformist in religion. He sat through the trials of the Jacobite lords in August 1746 and his attitude now seems somewhat callous, being diverted by anecdotes rather than moved by the real distress and possible injustice. There is almost no evidence of his going to church out of piety, though he did attend High Mass in Calais and in Genoa during his Grand Tour, seemingly out of curiosity. There are plenty of references in the letters to the consolations of religion at the time of death and evidence of his disapproval of free-thinkers, but no sign that he found in Church doctrine or ritual any interpretation of the predicament of his personal life.

A Summary

What sort of man, then, was Thomas Gray? "TG" to his friends, "Mr Gray" to his acquaintances, never, apparently, plain "Tom". He was a distant, private man, small in height, with intelligent, pleasant, regular features, plumpish as he grew older, with no great presence or charisma. He was kind and sympathetic to those who deserved it, acerbic and sarcastic to those who deserved the reverse. He had a quick and lively mind, a sensitive imagination, and a robust independence, but all was clouded by a frequently returning melancholia. He never quite achieved all that he might have done: he never became the fluent poet or the successful professor, never found a female friend, lost his closest male friend early in life, was forced to live on reserves of love left by his mother. But he remained a kindly, amusing individual, who left behind one great poem and one beautiful prose work, too little regarded.

Tailpiece: Gray's Will

First, I desire that my body may be deposited in the vault made by late dear mother in the church-yard of Stoke-Poges near Slough in Buckinghamshire, near her remains, in a coffin of season'd oak neither lin'd nor cover'd; and (unless it be very inconvenient) I would wish, that one of my Executors may see me laid in the grave, & may distribute among such honest & industrious poor persons in the said parish, as he thinks fit, the sum of ten pounds in charity.

[From Appendix X in Gray's Correspondence, p.1283]

Overleaf: The Lower End of Ullswater, by Joseph Farington

DAY ONE

Brough to Penrith

30 Sept: W^d at N: W. clouds & sunshine. a mile & ½ from Brough on a hill lay a great army encamp'd. to the left open'd a fine valley with green meadows & hedge-rows, a Gentleman's house peeping forth from a grove of old trees. on a nearer approach appear'd myriads of horses & cattle in the road itself & in all the fields round me, a brisk stream hurrying cross the way, thousands of clean healthy People in their best party-color'd apparel, Farmers & their families, Esquires & their daughters, hastening up from the dales & down the fells on every side, glittering in the sun & pressing forward to join the throng: while the dark hills, on many of whose tops the mists were yet hanging, served as a contrast to this gay & moving scene, wch continued for near two miles more along the road, and the crowd (coming towards it) reach'd on as far as Appleby.

On the ascent of the hill above Appleby the thick hanging wood & the long reaches of the Eden (rapid, clear, & full as ever) winding below with views of the Castle & Town gave much employment to the mirror: but the sun was wanting & the sky overcast. oats & barley cut everywhere, but not carried in. passed Kirby-thore, S^r W: Dalston's house at Acorn-bank, Whinfield-park, Harthorn-oaks, Countess-pillar, Brougham-Castle, Mr Brown (one of ye six Clerks) his large new house, cross'd the Eden & the Eimot (pronounce *Eeman*) with its green vale, & at 3 o'clock dined with Mrs Buchanan at *Penrith* on trout & partridge. in the afternoon walk'd up the *Beacon-hill* a mile to the top, saw Whinfield & Lowther-parks, & thro' an opening in the bosom of that cluster of mountains, wch the Doctor well remembers, the Lake of Ulz-water, with the craggy tops of a hundred nameless hills. these to W: & S:, to the N: a great extent of black & dreary plains, to E: *Cross-fell* just visible thro' mists & vapours hovering round it.

COMMENTARY

GRAY made two attempts to visit the Lake District in the company of his friend, Dr Thomas Wharton of Old Park, near Darlington. On the first attempt in August, 1767, they had got as far as Keswick, when Dr Wharton was taken ill in the night with asthma. According to a letter to Mason, they "went on however over stupendous hills to Cockermouth: here the Dr: grew still worse in the night, so we came peppering (&raining) back through Keswick to Penrith [.... and so over Stanemoor home". They tried again in September 1769 but again the doctor was ill. Gray describes what happened in a later letter to a Cambridge friend, James Brown.

> I set out on the 29th September, with poor Doctor Wharton, and lay at Brough, but he was seized with a fit of the asthma the same night, and obliged in the morning to return home. I went by Penrith to Keswick, and passed six days there, lap'd in Elysium; then came slowly by Ambleside to Kendal, and third day arrived here [Lancaster]. I now am projecting to strike across the hills into Yorkshire by Settle, and so get to Mason's; then, after a few days, I shall move gently towards Cambridge [10 Oct. 1769].

We owe the very existence of the journal therefore to this illness of Wharton's, for Gray kept it to let him know what he had missed.

The approach via Brough was a good one then but is a bad one now. Indeed, one could hardly choose a worse way of approaching the Lake District than by the A66. It is an evil road, with few safe stretches in which to overtake, beset by sightless bends and rises and falls, and stained and burnt by numerous appalling accidents. If you are local, you constantly remember places where children have died, cars have careered into walls, lorries have burst into flame. There are few experiences on any road worse than descending Stainmoor at a speed forced on one by a huge and heavy lorry close on one's tail, with blinding lights flashing into one's eyes, in the dark or in high wind or heavy rain. Villages like Kirby Thore and Temple Sowerby seem impossible to live in, such is the constant stream of high-speed traffic.

Gray was caught up in a different sort of congestion as he came down the hill towards Brough. He had timed his visit, presumably by chance, to coincide with the Brough Hill fair, one of the oldest cattle fairs in England, taking place then on 30th September and 1st October. William Hutchinson records that in those days, "the number of cattle exposed to sale, on an average, amounted to eight thousand and upwards, one thousand horses, together with a prodigious quantity of sheep". Michael ffinch, in his modern account of the Upper Eden valley, describes how, "The inns on the route made special provisions, great game pies were prepared, while the people of the surrounding villages would set up tables of nuts, apples, gingerbread, sweets, and dainties". No wonder Gray gives a picture of bustle and number and occasion. Its role, however, has now been taken over by Appleby fair in July and even that is now rather a sad and disorderly event.

Gray had come this way two years before, at the end of his first visit. He had then taken rather more notice of Appleby, when he had visited the church there on his way home and composed a parody of the Countess of Pembroke's epitaph on her mother on a tomb there.

Now clean, now hideous, mellow now, now gruff,
She swept, she hissed, she ripened and grew rough
At Broom, Pendragon, Appleby, and Brough.

Gray is referring, of course, to four of the castles which the Countess renovated. The formidable Lady Anne Clifford, "our good Countesse", as Gray later refers to her, seems to have been a standing joke between Wharton and Gray. It would not have been difficult for Gray to stop at the Countess's Pillar (though it is almost impossible to stop there now), as it is right beside the road. It was erected to mark the place where the good Countess paid a last farewell to her mother in 1656 and a service is still held there every year for the distribution of charity money.

It is not surprising that Gray should mark his progress by ticking off the names of landowners whose estates he was passing. Eighteenth-century maps gave the names of such gentlemen over the areas that they owned. Sir William Dalston's house at Acorn Bank lies some way off the road and its fine gardens are now in the ownership of the National Trust.

Whinfield Forest was an extensive estate, then belonging to the Earl of Thanet and now a huge holiday village. The Earl appears to have had no problem in combining the office of High Sheriff for Westmorland with his notorious keeping of the well-known courtesan, Nelly O'Brien (whose deceptively innocent eyes still shine out of the graceful portrait of her by Reynolds in the Wallace Collection). Gray, who had a satirical eye, appears not to have been provoked by this but there is perhaps a note of envy of the "large new house" at Brougham that had just been purchased by one of the Clerks of the Court of Chancery, a government sinecure abolished in 1843. Had Gray felt himself to be the social equal of any of these gentlemen, he might have called: his fame as the poet of the *Elegy* would have secured him an invitation. He was either too absorbed in his journey or, more probably, too conscious of his inferior social position. He mentions Mr Hudleston of Hutton St John and Mr Hassel of Dalemain on the next day with the same sort of submerged implication that these were people on whom he might have called. When he speaks of dining on trout and partridge with a Mrs Buchanan at Penrith at the unfashionable hour of 3 o'clock, the likelihood is that this a joke at his own expense, a droll comment on his social life, and that he was in fact sharing his dinner with the landlady at his inn.

It is also not surprising that Gray should have decided on a walk up Beacon Hill, since it dominates the town of Penrith, as well as the surrounding country. It is, however, a long, steep pull-up, especially if you walk all the way from the Market Place, as Gray probably did, and it would have taken him the best part of an hour. Even for the young William Hutchinson, when he made the same ascent a few years later, "the labour was great [even if] the view amply rewarded our fatigue". The path, in its later stages above the road, is now carefully laid out between barbed-wire fences, drained by runnels, guarded by keep-out notices and fire-warnings, and equipped to modern perfection with dog scoops. At the top is a square sandstone tower, erected fifty years before Gray's visit, in 1719. It is tapered off with a pyramid, and is hollow, with open arched windows and slits in the walls, surrounded with railings, which have failed to protect it from artistic as well as scrappy graffiti, some of it going back two hundred years. It is now seriously threatened by vandalism but it was possible in Gray's day to enter the tower and climb up to the first-floor windows: so Gray may well have had an all-round view. Now new plantations exclude the view to the harmless low hills to the north that depressed Gray, as well as the view east to Cross Fell. But one can still just see Ullswater, peeping through "the cluster of mountains", with Place Fell standing up clearly beside it. Jets now roar low overhead with great frequency, inter-city trains hoot as they leave Penrith station, the river of the M6 with its constant flow hums a couple of miles away below. A few years before Gray, Jacobite rebels halted on this spot, pondering an attack on Penrith but giving up the plan in headlong flight when they mistook a distant plantation for the pursuing Cumberland's troops; the plantation became known as "Wully's Black Horse". A few years later, the five-year-old Wordsworth stumbled upon a gibbet lower down the hill and the image of "the beacon crowning the low eminence" became the first of those "spots of time" that were to be so important to him.

TAILPIECE: GRAY'S EXPENSES 1767	
Expenses of journey into Cumberland with Dr: Wh:	9.9.0.
Black Cloathes	5.7.0.
Stockings, 2 pair	9.0.
Buckles & Buttons	1.3.
Post chaise to Old Park	7.6.
Advanced to Stephen	1.1.0.
Two Places in Yᵉ Coach	4.4.0.
Baggage over weight	11.3.
[From Gray's Notebook for 1767]	

Overleaf: Map of Roads between Penrith and Ullswater

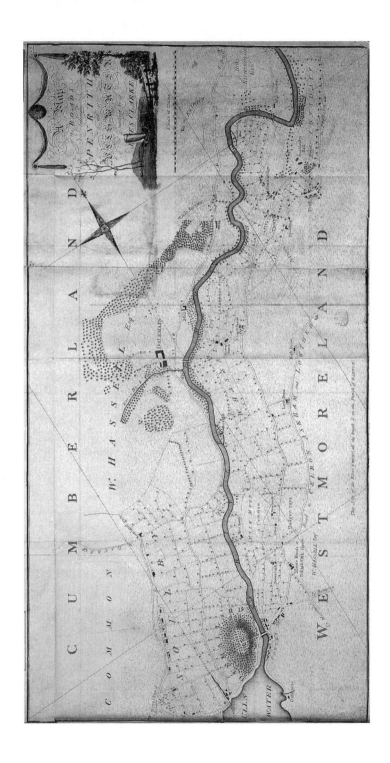

Day Two

Dunmallet and Ullswater

Oct:1. W^d at S: W: a grey autumnal day, air perfectly calm & gentle. went to see *Ulz-water* 5 miles distant. soon left the Keswick-road & turn'd to the left thro' shady lanes along the Vale of *Eeman*, wch runs rapidly on near the way, ripling over the stones. to the right is *Delmaine*, a large fabrick of pale red stone with 9 windows in front & 7 on the side built by Mr Hassel, behind it a fine lawn surrounded by woods & a long rocky eminence rising over them. a clear & brisk rivulet runs by the house to join the Eeman, whose course is in sight & at a small distance.

Farther on appears *Hatton St John*, a castle-like old mansion of Mr Huddleston. approach'd *Dunmallert*, a fine pointed hill, cover'd with wood planted by old Mr Hassle before-mention'd, who lives always at home & delights in planting. walk'd over a spungy meadow or two & began to mount this hill thro' a broad & strait green alley among the trees, & with some toil gain'd the summit. from hence saw the Lake opening directly at my feet majestic in its calmness, clear & smooth as a blew mirror with winding shores & low points of land cover'd with green inclosures, white farm-houses looking out among the trees, & cattle feeding. the water is almost every where border'd with cultivated lands gently sloping upwards till they reach the feet of the mountains, wch rise very rude & aweful with their broken tops on either hand. directly in front at better than 3 mile's distance *Place-Fell*, one of the bravest among them, pushes its bold broad breast into the midst of the Lake & forces it to alter it's course, forming first a large bay to the left & then bending to the right.

I descended *Dunmallert* again by a side avenue, that was only not perpendicular, & came to *Barton*-bridge over the *Eeman*, then walking thro' a path in the wood round the bottom of the hill came forth, where the *Eeman* issues out of the lake, & continued my way along it's western shore close to the water & generally on a level with it. saw a cormorant flying over it & fishing.

The figure of *Ulz-water* nothing resembles that laid down in our maps: it is 9 miles long, & (at widest) under a mile in breadth. after extending itself 3 m: & ½ in a line to S: W: it turns at the foot of *Place-Fell*, almost due West, and is here not twice the breadth of the Thames at London. it is soon again interrupted by the roots of *Helvellyn*, a lofty & very rugged mountain, & spreading again turns off to S: E:, & is lost among the deep recesses of the hills. to this second turning I pursued my way about four miles along its borders beyond a village scatter'd among trees & call'd *Water-malloch*, in a pleasant grave day, perfectly calm & warm, but without a gleam of sunshine: then the sky seeming to thicken, the valley to grow more desolate, & evening drawing on, I return'd by the way I came to *Penrith*.

COMMENTARY

DALEMAIN would have been the first item of interest on the road out of Penrith and is still much as Gray describes it: a classically symmetrical house in pink ashlar, with four windows to the left of the entrance, with its pillars and pediment, and four windows to the right and nine windows above. The lawn is now in front, sloping down to the road and a pretty little arched bridge over Dacre Beck, and the rear is now covered by gardens and trees. The house had been bought in 1680 by Sir Edward Hassel, chief steward to Gray's admired Lady Clifford. At the time of Gray's passing by, it was owned by Williams Hassel, who was indeed a great improver and planter of trees. A portrait of him by Arthur Devis in the house shows him in a pose very like Gainsborough's Mr Andrews, with his tricorne at a rakish angle; Gray, one imagines, must always have worn his tricorne spirit-level straight. It is a graceful and attractive house to visit, which one can do in the summer months now, and there are many fine objects from the eighteenth century, including a lovely engraved christening glass for Williams Hassel and a beautifully proportioned four-poster bed by Hepplewhite, with a message for Gray about the restorative power of sleep painted on its top-frame: *Curarum Dulce Levamen* ("the sweet alleviation of cares"). Gray would have been interested too in the unique Dalemain snowdrops (with three protruding inner petals) in the gardens, though it was, of course the wrong time of year.

It is curious that Gray should mention Hutton John at this point, as if it were the next thing to see along the road. Hutton John is a pele-tower, originally belonging to the Hudleston family, enlarged in the nineteenth century, now a private house, but it is three miles to the west along the Keswick road. Could Gray have seen it? I spent a long time checking this seemingly unimportant point, because my pursuit of Gray soon revealed that the countryside which he was looking at was quite different from the one I was looking at, even though the viewpoint might be the same. So many things have altered. Trees have been planted or have grown taller or have been felled, roads have altered their routes, lakes have been flooded or changed their water-levels, streams have altered their courses, walls have been built, the very air is less clear. What might have been visible two hundred years ago may not be visible now. Constantly I would find myself having to make mental adjustments for differences in physical scene or mental attitude which it is now very easy (but misleading) to ignore. In this case, I came to the conclusion that Hutton John, even then, would have been hidden by a low ridge. Possibly Gray spotted Dacre Castle instead, which *is* visible from a low hill just above the road, and later attributed the wrong name to it. Gray is not often wrong on details. He seems to have liked to identify the houses of old aristocratic families, probably out of antiquarian interest. He must have been looking out for this one and persuaded himself that he had seen it.

Dunmallet, a little further along the Ullswater road, is only 775 feet high and the top is less than a mile from the road. The most useful modern guidebook (Wainwright's *Outlying Fells of Lakeland*) dismisses it as "looking not at all suitable for a fell-walking expedition". The way to walk up it now is to park in the large car-park on the north side of the bridge, follow the path to the back of the wood, and then ascend the north slope. It is not very rewarding. The wood is a tangle of undergrowth, the path can be muddy, the top is covered in brambles and scrub and tightly packed trees. It is not possible to see anything of the surrounding countryside. There is no cairn to mark the summit.

It must have been very different in 1769. The trees were young Scotch firs but they were planted in a very regular fashion with three pathways leading to the top, which must itself have been clear. To obtain anything like the view that Gray saw, one now has to ascend Dunmallet's opposite number to the south, Heughscar Hill, a hill not much regarded by modern fell-walkers, though apparently well known to locals and pony-riders. One can easily walk up this low grassy limestone scarp from Roe head, above Pooley Bridge, and the reward is one of the finest views in the entire district. A grassy foreground leads to the lake in the middle distance, with Gowbarrow and Great Mell Fell beyond and the whole line of the Helvellyn range and Saddleback to the right as the skyline. These are not "nameless hills" to the modern walker nor are they "rude and aweful" but well-loved features of a friendly landscape. With Gray, however, something of the older attitudes still survives: the mountains have an air of impenetrability and are frequently spoken of as dark and fearful, as they had seemed to the likes of Defoe and Celia Fiennes.

Gray's path down Dunmallet is certainly steep. His description of it as "only not perpendicular" is a nicely humourous way of exaggerating it but detractors of Gray, who would accuse him of nervousness and old-maidishness, might be made to do the same descent themselves in leather-soled shoes after heavy rain. Since he mentions the "spongy" ground, one assumes that he was wearing shoes and that he would have had to pick his way. His detractors might also like to perform the full extent of the remaining six miles of Gray's walk. It is another mile, albeit on the level, from the bottom of Dunmallet to Barton Bridge, over more spongy fields. Gray does not make it clear whether he crossed the bridge but it seems more likely that he stayed on the same, western bank and walked back towards Ullswater. He then appears to have kept walking along the lake shore (where the road now runs) to some point beyond Watermillock, where he must have been picked up by his post-chaise. Not a hard walk by anyone's standards, ancient or modern, but a good one - without waterproof shoes or jacket, without a map or, it would seem, companion.

What Gray was wearing is more than a point of interest; it must have affected his mental outlook. He had bought a new black suit for his 1767 trip, two pairs of woollen stockings, and some spare buckles. He probably wore woollen knee-length breeches, shirt, neckerchief, long-sleeved wool waistcoat under a full-length (to the knees) great coat, with plenty of buttons and a silk-covered collar to turn up, if necessary. Most men of affluence, I am told, had several changes of underwear, especially shirts. Gray would also wear a tricorne, a round hat with the brim turned up on three sides, and probably carry a stout walking stick. His shoes would be leather, soles and uppers, fastened with a buckle, but not affording much protection to the ankles; they would be the weak point. He might also have had fustian gaiters; fustian is a combination of cotton and linen, soft, thick and flexible. Such an outfit might seem hopelessly inappropriate but, in fact, it would be warm and would shed the rain. What it would not do would be to give him the feeling of complete armour against all weathers that comes with a Goretex jacket, fell-boots, and rucksack with exposure bag, map, compass, whistle (or even mobile phone). The modern walker knows that he can laugh at the elements; Gray and his contemporaries could not do that and it is not surprising if they felt more vulnerable.

Gray's picture of Ullswater - "majestic in its calmness, clear & smooth as a blew mirror" - stays in the mind in its perfection, though the poet is practical enough to note the inaccuracies of his map. Kitchen delineates "Ulles Lake" as having a rectangular shape. The descendants of Gray's cormorants still fish in the lake, though the modern generation tend to sit idly around the islands, hanging their wings out to dry.

Overleaf: Derwentwater & Vale of Keswick, by Joseph Farington

DAY THREE

Penrith to Keswick

Oct:2. W^d at S:E:, sky clearing, *Cross-fell* misty, but the outline of the other hills very distinct. set out at 10 for *Keswick* by the road we went in 1767. saw *Greystock*-town & castle to the right, wch lie only 3 miles (over the Fells) from *Ulz-water*. pass'd through *Penradock*, & *Threlcot* [Threlkeld] at the feet of *Saddleback*, whose furrow'd sides were gilt by the noon-day Sun, while its brow appear'd of a sad purple from the shadow of the clouds, as they sail'd slowly by it. the broad & green valley of *Gardies* [Guardhouse] and *Low-side* with a swift stream glittering among the cottages & meadows lay to the left; & the much finer (but narrower) valley of St *John's,* opening into it: *Hill-top* the large, tho' low, mansion of the Gaskarths, now a Farm-house, seated on an eminence among woods under a steep fell, was what appear'd the most conspicuous, & beside it a great rock like some antient tower nodding to its fall. pass'd by the side of *Skiddaw* & its cub call'd *Latter-rig* [Latrigg], & saw from an eminence at two miles distance the Vale of Elysium in all its verdure, the sun then playing on the bosom of the lake, & lighting up all the mountains with its lustre.

Dined by two o'clock at the Queen's Head, & then straggled out alone to the *Parsonage*, fell down on my back across a dirty lane with my glass open in one hand, but broke only my knuckles: stay'd nevertheless, & saw the sun set in all its glory.

COMMENTARY

THE road from Penrith to Keswick has been re-routed many times over the years and the line which it follows now is very different from the one that it followed in Gray's day. It had recently been turnpiked and aimed to join up, rather than to by-pass, villages on the route. It left Penrith in a south-westerly direction to Stainton and then turned north-west to Penruddock and traversed what was then the unfenced open ground of Hutton Moor towards Threlkeld. Gray appears to have been fascinated by the place-names of all the places he passed through, "these barbarous names", as he rightly calls them, noting them down as spelt on his inaccurate, large-scale map (probably Kitchen's map of Cumberland, published in 1764). Part of the impact of a foreign landscape is the alien nature of the names and these names were mostly Norse in origin, with a few British survivals, all meaningless at first impact. Penruddock ("Penradock" on Gray's map) is one of the few British names but, while the "pen" element is common enough (meaning "chief"), the second half of the name is a mystery. Threlkeld has the genuine Norse ring about it and goes back to "Thrall's spring". Guardhouse is also Norse, meaning the "house of the garth", and Latrigg is a compound of two Norse words, each meaning hill. Gray's description of Latrigg as "the cub of Skiddaw" nicely sums up the relation of the outlying small hill to its parent massif.

The only way now to get anything of the feel of the approach to Keswick that Gray must have experienced is to take the minor road that still runs to the south of the A66. It is a switchback of a road with grass in the middle, narrow, between high hedges and dry-stone walls, over humpback bridges that threaten the under-side of a modern car, with blind corners and overhanging trees and gates that need to be opened and passing the ancient farmhouses that Gray passed, like Wallthwaite, with 1720 still just legible above its door lintel. The lane does not go all the way but it is worth leaving the main road for. It gives a thrill in a car; it must have been magical in a post-chaise.

It would have taken Gray about three hours to cover the distance that we now hurry over. He would have had more time for the "sad purple" of Saddleback and the Glenderamackin's "stream glittering among the cottages" to the south. The white farmstead of Hill Top still stands out clearly on its rocky knoll at the mouth of the valley, with the steep fell of Wallthwaite Crag behind it, if you can make time to look out for it. On the day on which I walked up the stony road to the farm, a lad was walking across the yard with a bucket. He claimed not to know anything about the history of the house - they had only been there a year - but he did know that there was an inscription on a cupboard in the front parlour of the house. He popped inside and soon emerged with the information that "IAG 1707" was carved over one of the cupboards: John and Anne Gaskarth, the owners in its halcyon days. Gray must have known to look out for it from his fellow-resident at Pembroke, Joseph Gaskarth, whose home it then was; he also seems to have known that the family was experiencing hard times. The house was sold a few years later to the acquisitive Lord Lonsdale. Gray's phrase about the huge rock next to it, "nodding to its fall", sounds like a quotation and indeed it is; it comes from Pope's *Essay on Man* and is meant to hint at a downfall due to fate. There is, however, no huge rock next to the farm now. What may have happened is that the farm may have been in the path of a huge amount of debris which came down this valley-side, as far down as Legburthwaite, in a terrific storm, described in *The Gentleman's Magazine* in 1755. Houses were washed away lower down the valley and Hutchinson later recorded how "the hand of God, in miraculous manner, stayed a rolling rock, in the midst of its dreadful course, which would have crushed the whole tenement [the village school] with its innocents". It is still possible to see some of the debris on the hillsides. Possibly Gray's rock was part of this debris and possibly it has since "nodded to its fall" and broken up in the fields below.

The old road took a completely different line in its approach to Keswick, keeping to the high ground to the south of the River Greta and coming past the stone circle on Castle-rigg. There is a good view of Keswick from here and to Gray it seems to have been like the first sight of a heaven on earth; it was the Vale of Elysium. Now the Vale of Elysium has a supermarket and housing estates and sodium street lights and untold tourist amenities. It is actually still a fine sight from the hills round about but the town does now sprawl away from its original cluster round the Moot-hall; a contemporary map shows fewer than 70 houses in the town at that time.

Gray understandably headed for the Queen's Head in the centre

of Keswick (now simply the Queen's), though he had stayed at the Royal
Oak in 1767. It must have been the premier tourist hotel, despite the
George's claim to greater seniority, since John Brown's early descriptive
guide to Keswick was advertised on its title page as being sold at the
Queen's Head and the inn later became the Keswick base for the
topographical painter, William Green, towards the end of the century. It
must have done too well in those days, for its front is now heavily
Victorian and nothing of its eighteenth-century character remains.

    Gray is not generous in detail about the logistics of his tour. It is
therefore hard to imagine him paying off the post-chaise, unpacking his
luggage, changing his shoes, ordering his meal, and then deciding to go
for an apparently aimless walk in the way freshly arriving tourists still do.
Gray, however, did have an aim: to reach the viewpoint he had visited in
1767, at the vicarage (now Crosthwaite Grange) near Crosthwaite
Church, a mile to the west of Keswick. Perhaps he was feeling travel-
weary when he says he "straggled out" alone or perhaps he is giving an
explanation for his fall. It must have been a blow to Gray's dignity to fall
on his back; quite how he grazed his knuckles in such a fall (since that is
all the word "broke" means) is not very clear. Vicarage Hill is no longer
a dirty lane but it does rise steeply and there is a good view from the top,
though the school next door has the best of it now. It would have been
much better then, when there were no other houses, and it became an
established view-point. West made it Station VIII in his guide and
narrowed down the position to the horsing-block in the Vicarage garden,
though characteristically he thought he knew of a better view from
Ormathwaite.

    To frame the view, Gray needed his Claude glass. He frequently
mentions this piece of equipment and it seems to have been an essential
item to the eighteenth-century tourist. It was a concave mirror made with
dark tinted glass; it could be oval or rectangular, small or relatively large
but always pocketable, like a cigarette case. One would think, from the
way that they are mentioned that they must have transformed a view into
something magical. In fact, they are rather disappointing. All that they
do is to allow one to compose a balanced picture, while the tinting has

the effect of removing detail and giving a sombre tone. To use the glass one has to turn one's back on the scene and look at its reflection. Norman Nicholson saw this as symbolical of the Picturesque movement's departure from reality and criticizes it in a poem, in which he imagines Gray looking at a scene in his glass and being tempted to look at the real view.

> What if I listen? What if I learn?
> What if I break the glass and turn
> And face the objective lake and see
> The wide-eyed stranger sky-line look at me.

Elsewhere Nicholson criticizes the Picturesque movement in very strong terms. "In the Picturesque, the only creative act is that of man himself, a small mean, self-satisfied manipulation of an abstract landscape." That meanness can surely not apply to Gray. He was prepared to put down his glass, as Nicholson himself admits, and look about "with a clarity of vision for which he has not often been credited". One has to see the Claude glass as a harmless toy or, at least, as no worse than a modern camera. There may be a touch of absurdity in the thought of Gray snapping out his glass at every view but it is certainly no more ridiculous than the sight of modern tourists trying to capture the ineffable at almost every curve in the road along almost every lake shore. Like them Gray was trying to spiritualize what he saw, to store away a mental image for memory's use, as Wordsworth recommended.

Overleaf: The Grange in Borrowdale, by Joseph Farington

DAY FOUR

Borrowdale

Oct: 3. W^d at S:E:, a heavenly day. rose at seven, & walk'd out under the conduct of my Landlord to *Borrodale*. the grass was cover'd with a hoarfrost, wch soon melted, & exhaled in a thin blewish smoke. crossed the meadows obliquely, catching a diversity of views among the hills over the lake & islands, & changing prospect at every ten paces, left *Cockshut,* & Castle-hill (wch we formerly mounted) behind me, & drew near the foot of *Walla-crag*, whose bare & rocky brow, cut perpendicularly down above 400 feet, as I guess, awefully overlooks the way: our path here tends to the left, & the ground gently rising, & cover'd with a glade of scattering trees & bushes on the very margin of the water, opens both ways the most delicious view, that my eyes ever beheld. behind you are the magnificent heights of *Walla*-crag; opposite lie the thick hanging woods of Ld Egremont, & *Newland*-valley with green & smiling fields embosom'd in the dark cliffs; to the left the jaws of *Borodale*, with that turbulent Chaos of mountain behind mountain roll'd in confusion; beneath you, & stretching far away to the right, the shining purity of the *Lake*, just ruffled by the breeze enough to shew it is alive, reflecting rocks, woods, fields, & inverted tops of mountains, with the white buildings of *Keswick*, *Crosthwait*-church, & *Skiddaw* for a back-ground at distance. oh Doctor! I never wish'd more for you; & pray think, how the glass played its part in such a spot, wch is called *Carf-close-reeds*: I chuse to set down these barbarous names, that any body may enquire on the place, & easily find the particular station, that I mean. this scene continues to *Barrow-gate*, & a little farther, passing a brook called *Barrow-beck*, we enter'd *Borodale*. the crags named *Lodoor-banks* now begin to impend terribly over your way; & more terribly, when you hear, that three years since an immense mass of rock tumbled at once from the brow, & and bar'd all access to the dale (for this is the only road) till they could work their way thro' it. luckily no one was passing at the time of this fall; but down the side of the mountain & far into the lake lie dispersed the huge fragments of this ruin in all shapes & in all directions. something farther we turn'd aside into a coppice, ascending a little in front of *Lodoor* water-fall. the height appears to be about 200 feet, the quantity of water not great, tho' (these three days excepted) it had rain'd daily in the hills for near two months before: but then the stream was nobly broken, leaping from rock to rock, & foaming with fury. on one side a towering crag, that spired up to equal, if not overtop, the neighbouring cliffs (this lay all in shade & darkness) on the other hand a rounder broader projecting hill shag'd with wood & illumined by the sun, wch glanced sideways on the upper part of the cataract. the force of the water wearing a deep channel in the ground hurries away to join the lake. we descended again, & pass'd the stream over a rude bridge. soon after we came under *Gowder-crag*, a hill more formidable to the eye & to the apprehension than that of *Lodoor*; the rocks atop, deep-cloven perpendicularly by the rains, hanging loose & nodding forwards, seem just starting from their base in shivers: the whole way down & the road on both sides is strew'd with piles of the fragments strangely thrown across each other & of a dreadful bulk. the place reminds one of those passes in the Alps, where the Guides tell you to move on with speed, & say nothing, lest the agitation of the air should loosen the snows above, & bring down a mass, that would overwhelm a caravan. I took their counsel here and hasten'd on in silence.

Non ragioniam di lor; ma guarda, e passa! [2]

The hills here are cloth'd all up their steep sides with oak, ash, birch, holly, &c: some of it has been cut 40 years ago, some within these 8 years, yet all is sprung again green, flourishing, & tall for its age, in a place where no soil appears but the staring rock, & where a man could scarce stand upright.

Met a civil young farmer overseeing his reapers (for it is oat-harvest here) who conducted us to a neat white house in the village of

---

2. "Let us not speak of them, but look, and pass on" - Dante, *The Inferno*, Canto 3, 1.51.

Grange, wch is built on a rising ground in the midst of a valley. round it the mountains form an aweful amphitheatre, & thro' it obliquely runs the Darwent clear as glass, & shewing under it's bridge every trout, that passes. beside the village rises a round eminence of rock cover'd entirely with old trees, & over that more proudly towers *Castle-crag*, invested also with wood on its sides, & bearing on its naked top some traces of a fort said to be Roman. by the side of this hill, wch almost blocks up the way, the valley turns to the left & contracts its dimensions, till there is hardly any road but the rocky bed of the river. the wood of the mountains increases & their summits grow loftier to the eye, & of more fantastic forms: among them appear *Eagle's-Cliff, Dove's-nest, Whitedale-pike*, &c: celebrated names in the annals of Keswick. the dale opens out about four miles higher till you come to *Sea-Whaite* (where lies the way mounting the hills to the right, that leads to the *Wadd-mines*) all farther access is here barr'd to prying Mortals, only there is a little path winding over the Fells, & for some weeks in the year passable to the Dale's-men; but the Mountains know well, that these innocent people will not reveal the mysteries of their ancient kingdom, the reign of Chaos & old Night. only I learn'd, that this dreadful road dividing again leads one branch to *Ravenglas*, & the other to *Hawkshead*.

For me I went no farther than the Farmer's (better than 4 m: from Keswick) at *Grange*: his Mother & he brought us butter, that Siserah would have jump'd at, tho' not in a lordly dish, bowls of milk, thin oaten-cakes, & ale; & we had carried a cold tongue thither with us. our Farmer was himself the Man, that last year plunder'd the Eagle's eirie: all the dale are up in arms on such an occasion, for they lose abundance of lambs yearly, not to mention hares, partridge, grous, &c: he was let down from the cliff in ropes to the shelf of rock, on wch the nest was built, the people above shouting & hollowing to fright the old birds, wch flew screaming round, but did not dare to attack him. he brought off the eaglet (for there is rarely more than one) & an addle egg. the nest was roundish & more than a yard over, made of twigs twisted together. seldom a year passes but they take the brood or eggs, & sometimes they shoot one, sometimes the other Parent, but the surviver has always found a mate (probably in Ireland) & they breed near the old place. by his description I learn, that this species is the *Erne* (the Vultur *Albicilla* of Linnaeus in his last edition, but in yours *Falco Albicilla*) so consult him & Pennant about it.

Walk'd leisurely home the way we came, but saw a new landscape: the features were the same in part, but many new ones were disclosed by the mid-day Sun, & the tints were entirely changed. take notice this was the best or perhaps the only day for going up Skiddaw, but I thought it better employ'd: it was perfectly serene, & hot as midsummer.

In the evening walk'd alone down to the Lake by the side of *Crow-Park* after sunset & saw the solemn colouring of night draw on, the last gleam of sunshine fading away on the hill-tops, the deep serene of the waters, & the long shadows of the mountains thrown across them, till they nearly touch'd the hithermost shore. at distance heard the murmur of many waterfalls not audible in the day-time. wish'd for the Moon, but she was *dark to me & silent, hid in her vacant interlunar cave.*

COMMENTARY

A HEAVENLY day, indeed! A miraculous day! Thank heaven that it did not rain! This is one of the great days in all travel literature - a model for both Dorothy and William Wordsworth later, and for Coleridge, and for all writers who would write a journal.

It seems safe to say that only a few exceptional tourists now get up at 7 to go for a walk. Not many actually walk from Keswick to Grange and back, when it is so quick in the car. Not many see those early morning or late evening demonstrations of natural strangeness and beauty, such as that delicate moment when the October frost "exhaled in a thin blewish smoke". What distinguishes Gray's travel-writing, and indeed all good travel-writing, is this ability to make short phrases count. Wordsworth picked out this quality when he commended Gray's *Journal* for its "distinctness and unaffected simplicity". Yet this poet, who claimed that "the language of the age is never the language of poetry", was nevertheless capable of the reverse, of making his prose poetic. Indeed, he apologizes in one of his letters for a sentence that is "so fine [...] you must translate it into prose". That, of course, is impossible with a visionary phrase like the one describing Derwentwater, "the shining purity of the lake". Gray's entranced relationship to the scene, the sacramental quality that he wanted and drew from it, as well as the lake's calm reflection at a pictorial level, are all there. It is worth comparing the phrase with Coleridge's (exaggerated?) description of the same autumnal scene as "a cauldron of melted silver boiling". You pays your money and you makes your choice - or you make room for both styles.

Another of Gray's techniques is his habit of attaching personal names to places; they almost always mean that he felt some personal connection, however slight. "Lord Egremont's woods" belonged to George Wyndham, the third earl, who was only 12 when he succeeded to the peerage and would be only 17 or 18 at this time. Gray would certainly know of him and would probably have met him in London. He became a remarkably generous man of great wealth, a patron of the arts and an agricultural improver.

It was a sense of wonder similar to Gray's reaction to the mist rising which had sent a clergyman called John Brown, more adventurously than Gray, to the top of Walla Crag a few years previously to experience the uncanny quiet which descended after sunset and twilight and the extraordinary transforming light of a full moon over the panorama of the central mountains. Brown's poem, originally written to be included with a prose description of the lake, is worth quoting in full because it contains the same imaginative reaction to the magical qualities of landscape, though different in the angle and timing of its viewpoint.

> Now sunk the Sun, now Twilight sunk, and Night
> Rode in her zenith; nor a passing breeze
> Sighed to the groves, which in the midnight air
> Stood motionless, and in the peaceful floods
> Inverted hung: For now the billow slept
> Along the shore, nor heav'd the deep, but spread
> A shining mirror to the moon's pale orb,
> Which, dim and waining, o'er the shadowy clifts,
> The solemn woods and spiry mountain-tops

Her glimmering faintness threw: Now every eye
Oppress'd with toil, was drown'd in deep repose;
Save that the unseen shepherd in his watch,
Propt on his crook, stood listn'ng by the fold,
And gaz'd the starry vault and pendant moon;
Nor voice nor sound broke on the deep serene,
But the soft murmur of swift-rushing rills,
Forth-issuing from the mountain's distant steep
(Unheard till now, and now scarce heard) proclaim'd
All things at rest, and imag'd the still voice
Of quiet whispering to the ear of Night.

My wife and I tried to replicate the experience of this poem one night in
July, when the sunset was followed by the rise of a full moon: you also
need a clear sky and no wind. We got the identical conditions (plus
midges) but not the uncanny silence, in which Brown felt he could hear
the quiet whispering of streams as if it were a presence. You have to go
further into the mountain heart to get this degree of silence now.

It is easy to mock Gray for his refusal to leave the valley and
ascend the crag as Brown did and to ridicule his reactions to the steep
rocks and higher mountains and valley recesses as excessive or neurotic.
Of course, he was apprehensive and we are not, but he was no fool and,
if the emotional impact on us is less than it was on him, we are the losers.
Gray rarely exaggerates but he does use a different language. Words like
"awefully" and "terribly", "formidable" and "dreadful", are now empty
intensives but they then had more exact meanings. In particular, the
word "horror" had a specific meaning, now obsolete, of "a feeling of awe
or reverent fear (without any suggestion of repugnance); a thrill of awe
or of imaginative fear" (OED). What Gray is trying to convey here is a
reaction which has now largely dropped out of our experience, at least in
the Lake District, but which was nevertheless real and not exaggerated.
It is the experience that Wordsworth is trying to describe in his accounts
of nutting and skating and of the stolen boat and it is a valuable
experience, worth recapturing. It will not do to mock these feelings,

though it is understandable that the effect now is of exaggeration. There are other reasons for Gray's more heightened reaction. It has to be remembered that the physical geography itself was different. The road to Grange was narrow and rough, and beyond Grange it was impossible to travel by wheeled vehicles. There had recently been severe storms and serious rockfalls as a result of them. The eighteenth-century usage of the word "shivers" - actually meaning small pieces of rock - now also serves to convey some of Gray's apprehension. One also has to bear in mind that some of the writers immediately following Gray felt an animus towards him, expressed in scorn. Samuel Rogers, for example, reporting at third hand ten years later, accused Gray of being "difficult to be pleased". Others mocked his inability to ride and his apparent reluctance to go on the lake or to ascend Skiddaw. He would have his own reasons, however, for not wishing to join in what were already the regular tourist excursions and he was not unadventurous in his own way: he did walk on his own at times, without a map in some wild places.

Gray is, for example, quite right in estimating the "magnificent heights" of Walla Crag as being above 400 feet and it is still, even to modern eyes, an impressive line of crags as one goes further south past Falcon Crag, Shepherds Crag and the "more formidable" Gowder Crag. It is ironic that these crags have become notable and popular rock-climbing areas, for rock-climbing is surely the ultimate destination of the pursuit of fear in a protected environment, a cult of difficulty and danger on steep rock minimized by rope and belay technology that would have shocked and appalled Gray. I have hung here myself, on a climb absurdly called Donkey's Ears, and can testify to the full "horror" of the situation.

Lodore Falls, which Gray turned aside to see, was clearly already a tourist sight to be seen. Part of its fame may be due to the Reverend John Dalton, whose poem on the falls, published in 1755, must have attracted attention to it, though one must assume that Dalton himself was taken there (perhaps by John Brown) because of an existing reputation going back maybe another ten years. Dalton's motivation in the poem is curious, curious because his poem has a double, linked subject, the mines at Whitehaven as well as the falls, each of equal interest to Dalton, and curious because of his cultivated taste for armchair horror, significantly different from a true sense of awe. His poem has originality for its day but no depth or freshness of detail in comparison with either Brown or Gray.

Let other streams rejoyce to roar
Down the rough rocks of dread Lodore,
Rush raving on with boisterous sweep,
And foaming rend the frighted deep,
Thy gentle Genius shrinks away
From such a rude unequal fray;
Thro' thine own native dale, where rise
Tremendous rocks amid the skies,
Thy waves with patience slowly wind,
Till they the smoothest channel find,
Soften the horrors of the scene,
And thro' confusion flow serene.
     HORRORS like these at first alarm,
But soon with savage grandeur charm
And raise to noblest thought the mind:
Thus by thy fall, Lodore, reclin'd,
The craggy cliff, impendent wood,
Whose shadows mix o'er half the flood,
The gloomy clouds, which solemn sail,
Scarce lifted by the languid gale
O'er the cap'd hill, and darken'd vale;
The ravening kite, and bird of Jove,
Which round th'aerial ocean rove,
And floating on the billowy sky,
With full extended pennons fly,
Their flutt'ring or their bleating prey
Thence with death-dooming eye survey;
Channels by rocky torrents torn,
Rocks to the lake in thunder born,
Or such as o'er our heads appear
Suspended in their mid-career,
To start again at His command,

Who rules fire, water, air, and land,
I view with wonder and delight,
A pleasing tho' an awful sight....

Torrents appear to have fascinated the later eighteenth century. It is possible now to examine word usage by means of reference to a collection of English poetry on compact disk and it appears from this that the word itself, "torrent", is used 365 times from 1750 to 1800, as opposed to only 151 times in the corresponding half of the seventeenth century. It is a crude statistic, with a number of untested variables, but it gives some indication of a new interest in wild water, as part of the new interest in wild scenery. Lodore lives now on its past fame, since it is rarely as impressive as it appears in eighteenth-century prints, except after heavy rain. Indeed, the way to visit it now is to save it for a wet day and go in the launch to the nearby landing stage. The path up to it is clearly marked (behind the big hotel) and there is shelter from the trees. If disappointed, there is another fall in Ashness Gill, up the fellside from Ashness Bridge, but to get there requires hard work and fell-boots.

The scene at Grange which follows the visit to Lodore is a warmly pleasing one: the kindly hospitality of the young farmer and his mother, the shared provisions, the chat about the crops, the names of the hills round about, the wad mines, the tall tales about robbing the eagle's nest. It is hard to see Gray in this setting as being "peevish", as Samuel Rogers claimed. He seems to have delighted in the company and they must have warmed to him. Food was one way to his heart, for he was always interested in good food, though careful with his digestion, making notes of new recipes, which he must have tried out from time to time as an amateur cook. The witty Biblical reference to Siserah - "She brought forth butter in a lordly dish" - at once compliments the farmer's wife and apologizes for her homely domestic ware. The farm-made butter was clearly delicious, the thin oat-cakes must have been new to him, the cold tongue seems more like the normal gentleman's picnic.

The story of robbing the eagle's nest seems authentic. There certainly were eagles, as the place-names of local crags make clear, and the attitude towards them seems much the same as Scots gamekeepers now: a perhaps exaggerated belief in the number of lambs they would kill. It is ironic that such strenuous efforts are now being made to re-introduce eagles into the Lake District. Gray was a keen observer, as the details about the nest, the eggs, and the number of young makes clear. He exchanged notes about birds and flowers with Gilbert White and Thomas Pennant and had his own copy of Linnaeus's *Systema Naturae*, which he carefully annotated. The classifications were still in a state of flux, as were the names, and it is not surprising that Gray's identification is not correct. Pennant classified the "erne", which Linnaeus had wrongly ranked with vultures, as a white-tailed eagle, supposedly inferior in size to a golden eagle; an immature golden eagle might well have white patches on its tail. Pennant curiously warns that "it is very unsafe to leave infants in places where eagles frequent". The place-names that Gray notes - Eagle's-cliff, Dove's Nest and Whitedale Pike - can have meant little to him as places. Eagle Crag is further down Borrowdale and Dove's Nest is now better known as a curious cave on the slopes of Glaramara, while Whitedale Pike seems to be a mishearing, perhaps for Grisedale Pike. But they have a resonance for him as celebrated in local history. Gray refers later, in his entry for 7th October, to the wad (or plumbago) mines in Borrowdale. One of the reasons why he may have been discouraged from going further up the valley could have been a desire on the part of the locals to keep prying eyes away from this buried treasure, though Bishop Nicholson had managed to visit them as early as 1710 and George Smith, after one unsuccessful attempt, eventually visited them in 1751, writing an article for *The Gentleman's Magazine*. William Wilberforce (the anti-slavery campaigner) met this same young farmer, Caleb Fisher as he named him, ten years later, and it would appear that Fisher continued to tell tales of Gray's visit for a long time afterwards into his old age.

        The criticism of Gray's alleged lack of daring and tendency to exaggerate, mentioned earlier, has particularly focussed on his exaltation of Sty Head Pass into a "dreadful road", only passable for some weeks in the year. It is not surprising that this should seem ridiculous when hundreds daily cross it now but the passage needs to be read with some attempt to see the situation through eighteenth-century eyes. William Rollinson, for instance, quoting this passage in his important *History of Man in the Lake District* (1967), concludes that Gray must have been "a timorous man" and "essentially a gullible person". While this is understandable in a modern context, it is unjust to dismiss Gray in these terms: "timorous" implies fearfulness to the point of cowardice and "gullible" implies a lack of intelligence. Before debunking Gray, it is important to remember, as Norman Nicholson warns us, that "we are dealing with a brilliant intellect, with a man of subtle and unending humour". He would not easily be hoodwinked. His map would give him no further information and he would have no reason to doubt what he was told, which was probably that Sty Head was a dangerous route, only passable in good weather. That judgement would have been standard at least until 1810. Part of what is happening here, however, is that Gray is wanting to believe in hidden places, accessible only to native people, an understandable form of primitivism. He is also going back in his mind to that Alpine pass that he crossed in 1739 and wanting the same sensation. Hence the earlier reference to Dante and the reference here to Milton's *Paradise Lost,* for the scale is epic. The word "chaos", frequent in the early writers (and already used earlier in the passage), suggests the forces of primal creation which he is sensing here, while the word "amphitheatre", also in constant use by the early writers, suggests a dramatic scene in which the onlooker is involved. Familiarity, however, has bred a kind of blindness in us. We now need immensity to "give us a buzz".

Gray's walk home makes a valuable point about walking in the Lake District: that there is nothing wrong with returning in the afternoon by the same route as that taken in the morning, because the tints and shadows are different, presenting a new landscape.

Gray had a particular purpose in completing his day by walking alone to Crow Park after sunset. It is clear from the verbal references that he makes that he was copying the advice given by Dr John Brown (whose poem on the Vale of Keswick has already been quoted) in his *Description of the Lake at Keswick,* published after the author's death in 1767. This suggests that "a walk by still moonlight (at which time the distant waterfalls are heard in all their variety of sound) among these inchanting dales opens a scene of such delicate beauty, repose, and solemnity, as exceeds all description". Gray succeeded in hearing the waterfalls but not in seeing the moon, which was hid in "her vacant interlunar cave", presumably because Gray had not hit on the right phase of the moon when it was full or perhaps because it was a cloudy night. Gray was a very allusive writer and there is more than an allusion to Milton here; Gray also seems to be quoting a phrase from the poem by John Brown (printed earlier), which was apparently originally written to form a part of the prose *Description*. The poem uses the unusual phrase "deep serene" and draws attention to the waterfalls "unheard by day". The curious thing is that this poem had not been published and that Gray must, therefore, have seen the original manuscript. That would not have been impossible in the eighteenth century, when it was common for literary works to circulate among a wide circle in manuscript, but the detailed allusion suggests that this manuscript had made a forceful impact on Gray and that it may have been the inspiration for his visit to Keswick.

It is ironic that all this area to the south of Keswick - Crow Park, Cockshut Wood, Friar's Crag - which made such an impact on Gray, has suffered seriously from mass tourism. The memorials to Rawnsley and Ruskin on the road to Friar's Crag tell the story of the revelation of a spirit in the universe. The immediately felt presence, however, is of areas of tarmac, parking restrictions, fences, seats, litter, graffiti, public conveniences, pleasure-boats, tea-gardens, and now a theatre. The National Trust has done its best to purchase and to preserve from further building encroachment but even this has meant discreet little notices, wooden side rails, constructed paths, appeals for money. If you raise your eyes to the hills at Friar's Crag or Crow Park and turn your back on the town, something survives. If you walk down in the early morning or late in the evening or choose a wet winter's day when no-one is about, something survives. For many people on a day trip, this is their experience of the Lake District. For many people it is not realistic to expect that they should put on boots and get further into the wilderness.

But what they are getting is not horror or immensity, even if they do get a slightly tawdry beauty.

TAILPIECE: GRAY THE NATURALIST (1)

April 2.[1763] Standard-Abricot, & Wall-Pears flower. Quince, Apple, and Sweet-briar in leaf. Currant flowers. Dutch-Elm opens its leaf.

4. Plumb in leaf.

5. Crown Imperial fl:

6. Plumb flowers. Hawthorn, Horse-chestnut, Mountain-Ash, in leaf.

9. Lime-Tree in leaf. Jonquil & single Anemone flower. Lady-birds seen.

11. Cowslip flowers, & Auricula. Swallow appears. Young Rooks caw in the nest.

14. Red-Start appears. Cherries in full bloom.

15. Frontignac Vine in leaf. Double Wall-flower blows.

16 Nightingale sings. Apple blossoms.

19. Chaffinch & Red-Start sit on their eggs.

20. Elm, Willow, & Ash, in flower (with the Black-Thorn) Hawthorn in full leaf.

21. Sycomore quite green. Oak puts out.

[From letter to Dr Wharton, August 1763]

Overleaf: Derwentwater towards Borrodale, by William Bellers.

DAY FIVE

Crow Park & Cockshut Hill

Oct: 4. W^d E:, clouds & sunshine, & in the course of the day a few drops of rain. Walk'd to *Crow-park*, now a rough pasture, once a glade of ancient oaks, whose large roots still remain on the ground, but nothing has sprung from them. if one single tree had remain'd, this would have been an unparallel'd spot, & Smith judged right, when he took his print of the Lake from hence, for it is a gentle eminence, not too high, on the very margin of the water & commanding it from end to end, looking full into the *gorge* of *Borodale*. I prefer it even to *Cockshut*-hill, wch lies beside it, and to wch I walked in the afternoon: it is cover'd with young trees both sown and planted, oak, spruce, scotch-fir, &c: all wch thrive wonderfully. there is an easy ascent to the top, & the view far preferable to that on Castle-hill (wch you remember) because this is lower & nearer to the Lake: for I find all points, that are much elevated, spoil the beauty of the valley, & make its parts (wch are not large) look poor & diminutive. while I was here, a little shower fell, red clouds came marching up the hills from the east, & part of a bright rainbow seem'd to rise along the side of Castle-hill.

From hence I got to the *Parsonage* a little before Sunset, & saw in my glass a picture, that if I could transmitt to you, & fix it in all the softness of its living colours, would fairly sell for a thousand pounds. this is the sweetest scene I can yet discover in point of pastoral beauty. the rest are in a sublimer style.

COMMENTARY

GRAY seems not to have realized that it usually rains in the Lake District and that he could not afford to have a lazy day. As an earlier explorer, Archibald Bower, put it in a letter written in 1755: "they have scarce three fine days there in 30 years, at least together". Gray, however, seems to have been extraordinarily fortunate in his spell of weather. He had all sorts: showers, sunshine, some unusual east winds, frost, warmth, but not the steady driving rain which can ruin a Lakes holiday.

Crow Park is not far to walk but it gave Gray what he wanted - the view he must have already seen in a print by Thomas Smith of Derby. Smith's print shows some very steep-sided mountains down in Borrowdale and a number of treeless islands in the lake and a foaming waterfall at Lodore under a lowering sky with heavy black clouds. Smith also shows one tree, hardly an oak, and the stumps of a number of others. The stumps are the remains of the oaks of the Jacobite Earl of Derwentwater, himself hanged after the 1715 rising, and his trees being likewise executed after the 1745. Another extant but earlier and anonymous print, now in the possession of Dove Cottage but originally painted for the Speddings of Mirehouse, shows the trees being felled. William Bellers' print from this viewpoint is also interesting and attractive in a different style: more gently pastoral, though with craggy and inaccurately drawn hillshapes and a similarly foaming waterfall at Lodore and with some suitably idle gentlemen and a lady sauntering in the foreground, oblivious to the view. Both Bellers and Smith seem to have been active in the area in the 1750s, before the writers got to work, and Smith's work, in particular, seems to have influenced Gray, since he mentions him again at Gordale Scar. Gray must have bought copies of the prints and been fascinated by their dramatic vision. Smith's landscape prints, some of them dating from the early 1740s, were the pioneers in popularizing mountain prospects, with their precipices and cascades, and it was Smith's eye which picked out what were later to become the classic views. Along with Brown's *Description of the Lake at Keswick*, Smith's engravings must have given Gray the initial urge to make this journey and must have determined at least some points on his route, as Farington's, Girtin's, Turner's and those of countless others would later be determined by Gray's.

Another picture attributed to this decade, though it must have come later, is the one by Anthony Devis in Abbot Hall Gallery, Kendal. It shows Skiddaw, with its summit wreathed in mists, from Calf Close Bay with a small boat in the foreground. The boat contains half-a-dozen obedient tourists sitting expectantly at attention, while a man in the bows prepares to fire a rifle - presumably to create an echo. This kind of activity must have come later in the 60s or 70s and the dates of the artist's life also make it likely that the painting has a later date than that ascribed to it on the frame. Nevertheless, it is a fine local example of early mountain landscape.

Gray continually refers to trees. It was an age for both felling and planting. Local newspapers a few years later have advertisements for the sale of oak woods in Borrowdale and alongside Derwentwater: "2358 full-grown oak trees [....] standing in that part of the estate called Far Park" and again "upwards of 400 oak trees together with a large quantity of ash standing and growing on Castle-bank". Fortunately they were also being replaced. Another advertisement by a John Sander, nurseryman, at Keswick, wishes to inform the public that "he has ready for sale a large quantity of Scotch-firs, from one-year-old to four, a great number of oaks, ashes, elm and beech". He would find it more difficult to make his living in that manner now. Gilbert White's diary at Selborne shows the same kind of contemporary interest in the nurturing and enjoyment of fine trees. It is a cheering thought that the oak trees growing now in Cockshut Wood were there in Gray's day, since it is said that an oak is 300 years growing, 300 years standing still, and 300 years dying. With trees one enters a different perspective on time and, in this case, a different concept of value. Gray would be seeing these trees as the frames of houses and ships, in terms of economic value as well as environmental heritage.

Gray is fond of the word "eminence", which he seems to use to denote the kind of low hill that he preferred. Whether he is right that "gentle eminences" give the best views is perhaps a matter of taste, though it is true that summit views do tend to flatten the panorama. In this case, Gray is comparing two low hills and, for most people now, the view from Castle-head, as it is now known, is incomparably finer than that from Cockshut Wood, where fully grown timber now excludes the view. Gray was beginning the eighteenth-century taste for "stations", select viewpoints giving balanced, composed pictures. The word, with its religious associations, seems already to have acquired its special tourist significance. We may not use the word any more but it would not be difficult to compose a list of tourist viewpoints - from Ashness Bridge or from the head of Windermere to the Langdale Pikes, for example - which still have a special status, re-appearing regularly in Lake District calendars. The obsession with summits, however, came later: Coleridge would seem to be the first who had to get to the top of everything.

Gray's final words for this day - "This is the sweetest scene I can yet discover in point of pastoral beauty" - are cut in a curious angular script into the slabs on the low wall running along the terrace of the old vicarage at Crosthwaite (now a private house). Canon Rawnsley had this done when he moved into the vicarage in 1883, presumably as a tribute to Gray's influence upon him. As Rawnsley was later one of the founders of the National Trust (in 1895), one might claim credit for Gray for bringing about, not only an appreciation of mountainous scenery, but also the consequent desire to protect it. Ironically, whereas Rawnsley was probably inspired by the mountain top skyline of Causey Pike and Grisedale Pike above him, it would seem from Gray's reference to "pastoral beauty" that he was looking at the pattern of farms and fields and woods and streams below him. There are two aesthetic categories being confused here by Rawnsley, though not by Gray. Gray is referring to the (to him) traditional Addisonian definition of beauty, a limited concept based on proportion and scale and form. He is clearly well aware also of the (to him) newer Burkean concept of "the sublimer style", which he had seen in Borrowdale. What Gray is not aware of is any notion of a third style, of the Picturesque, in which a view might be related to the rules of art or changed in its composition to suit the viewer.

TAILPIECE: GRAY THE NATURALIST (2)

April 20 [1760] Th: at 60. W^d S:W: Skylark, Chaffinch, Wren, & Robin singing. Horse-Chestnut, Wild-Bryar, Bramble, and Sallow had spread their leaves. Hawthorn & Lilac had formed their blossoms. Black-thorn, double-flowered Peach, & Pears in full bloom; Double Jonquils, Hyacinths, Anemones, single Wall-flowers, & Auriculas in flower. In the fields, Dog-Violets, Daisies, Dandelion, Buttercups, Red-Archangel, & Shepherd's Purse.

May 11. Very fine. W^d N:E: Horse-Chestnut in full bloom. Wall-nut and Vine spread. Lilacs, Persian Jasmine, Tulips, Wall-flowers, Pheasant-Eye, Lilly in the Valley in flower. In the fields, Furze, Cowslips, Hare-bells, & Cow-Parsnep.

[From a letter to Dr Wharton c.20 June 1760]

Overleaf: Derwentwater and Skiddaw, by Joseph Farington

Day Six

Derwentwater & Castlerigg

Oct: 5. W^d N: E: Clouds & sunshine. Walk'd thro' the meadows & corn-fields to the Derwent & crossing it went up *How-hill.* it looks along Bassinthwaite-water & sees at the same time the course of the river & a part of the Upper-Lake with a full view of Skiddaw. then I took my way through Portingskall village to the *Park,* a hill so call'd cover'd entirely with wood: it is all a mass of crumbling slate. pass'd round its foot between the trees & the edge of the water & came to a Peninsula that juts out into the lake & looks along it both ways. in front rises Walla-Crag, & Castle-hill, the Town, the road to Penrith, Skiddaw & Saddleback. returning met a brisk & cold N: Eastern blast, that ruffled all the surface of ye lake and made it rise in little waves that broke at the foot of the wood. After dinner walk'd up the Penrith-road 2 miles or more & turning into a corn-field to the right, call'd Castle-Rigg, saw a Druid-Circle of large stones 108 feet in diameter, the largest not 8 feet high, but most of them still erect: they are 50 in number. the valley of Naddle appear'd in sight, and the fells of *St. John's,* particularly the summits of *Catchidecam* (called by Camden, *Casticand*) & *Helvellyn* said to be as high as *Skiddaw,* & to rise from a much higher base. a shower came on, & I return'd.

COMMENTARY

THE shortish entry for this day is misleading. Gray covered about twelve to thirteen miles in distance, mostly on the flat on what were probably good paths, it is true, and he must have been walking, in two spells, for a total of seven or eight hours. When I repeated this walk, used as I am to fell-walking, I was tired and footsore at the end. The idea that Gray was physically feeble is clearly a nonsense. He may not have been as adventurously physical in his walking as Coleridge seems to have been, but he was energetic in distance and enterprising about finding his way.

Gray makes it seem as if he stepped out of the front door of the Queen's into a meadow. One now runs the gamut of a strange series of tourist shops before one can get to anything like a meadow and even then some of these green fields now sprout rugby posts or are bounded by high road embankments. Whatever bridge spanned the Derwent in Gray's day has long since gone and is now replaced by an attractive suspension bridge, carrying a footpath only, since the main road is now re-routed to the north. Battles have been fought over the Derwent bridges at this point, with Canon Rawnsley apparently triumphant in preserving the old bridge in the early 1900s but defeated after his death by a storm in the 1950s, which washed that bridge away. The new bridge may be out of character but it sways and creaks musically. On the other side of the Derwent a path to the right leads north along the river bank under another fine bridge, this one a graceful arch of blue slate, on towards another bigger concrete span carrying the A66. There is no subterranean way of avoiding this monster: you have to climb over the crash barriers and run across the asphalt no-man's land to the safety of the far side. Life becomes pastoral again and the path makes its way past another crossing-point, this time the abandoned and broken girder bridge of the old railway, to a stile below How farm. Here it is possible to scramble up to the top of the hill and share the view with the roosters from the farm below. Low though this hill is, it is raised above the river flats between the two lakes of Derwentwater and Bassenthwaite and, as Gray must have been told, it affords a good view of the swiftly running Derwent, of the upper part of Bassenthwaite, and of the massive front of Skiddaw. A Victorian house tops the hill a little aggressively; an old farm nestles below it more comfortably on the west side. A short walk through scruffy lanes brings one back across the A66 to Portinscale, now bigger than eighteenth-century Keswick must have been, with its original cottages, many of them turned into holiday homes, surrounded by more Victorian villas, modern bungalows, and guesthouses. The name Portinscale means "prostitute's hut" in one interpretation but there is no longer any obvious evidence of this activity: it all looks and feels very respectable.

Gray seems to have been able to follow the lake shore from here: this is no longer possible. Now one must follow the road past the Derwentwater Marina, with its Chartroom Bar, to Nichol End boatyard, with its beached armada of sailing boats of different shapes and sizes and more or less nautical names. A signed path leads through fenced-off private property, mostly woodland, towards the looming shape of Cat Bells. It seems to be a popular walk with young families, though there is not much open view to recommend it; perhaps people just want to be in the open air on a rough track and don't ask for too much more. At Hawse End, an outdoor pursuits centre, the path improves, leading pleasantly down through oak-dotted meadows to the lake and a little promontory overlooking Otterbield Bay. This seems to have been Gray's furthest point. Quite why he turned back here is not clear but probably it was the need to be back in Keswick for dinner at 2, or thereabouts. Did he have sandwiches in his pocket or even a woollen scarf to put on when the wind turned into a chilly north-east, blowing into his face on his return? Gray refuses to fill in all the blanks, just as he refuses to use the first person pronoun overmuch. The wind doesn't seem to have worried him unduly, any more than the rain did later in the day. He got his view, both ways, up and down the lake, and across to Walla Crag, though how he managed to pick out the Penrith Road from that distance is a problem. It was either a very clear day or Gray had remarkably good eyesight.

He must also have been strong-minded, or just keen to make the most of his time, to set off after dinner, at 3 or 4 o'clock to walk out of Keswick up the old road to Castlerigg. It is now a most unpleasant exercise along narrow sidewalks, with the River Greta on one side and a straggle of houses, fire-station, pubs, guesthouses, garage on the other. The traffic is constant; the plethora of road-signs amazing. At Chestnut Hill, a mile from the Queen's, one can turn off the main roads up towards Fieldside on a narrow unclassified road, eventually leaving the kerbstones and yellow lines behind for a wall-banked lane with a fine view over the valley of the Greta to Skiddaw and Saddleback. It is quite a pull-up, this road, and it does not really level out until one gets to Castlerigg itself and the lay-bys to the left of the square field enclosing the stone-circle.

It is not, of course, a druid's circle but, although it has been more accurately dated to the Stone Age, its original purpose has not been discovered. Gray is quite right in his numbering of the stones to 50 but the cornfield is now a green meadow owned by the National Trust. What they now have to be preserved against is tourist erosion. The site is gated and currently re-seeded and under constant attack by visitors, some of whom have little respect. Presumably, if this were Ayers Rock, there would be local inhabitants reminding us of the sacredness of this special religious place. Because we live in what seems at times the most secular of all countries, such a concept appears to be impossible. It is interesting that Gray should mention Camden's spelling of Catchedicam. Gray could have verified and compared the place-names with his copy of Camden on his return to Cambridge, since the journal was copied into letter form at a later date, except that the original notebooks also have the Camden references; Gray must have looked them up before he left and carried the information in his head! It is interesting too that Gray should have even spotted Catchedicam, since most walkers now would regard it as a subsidiary outlier of Helvellyn. It does have a distinctive pointed shape to match its poetically-sounding name and it seems to have caught Gray's eye, perhaps because Camden thought it one of the highest hills in England. He was lucky to have a clear day, as did Keats some thirty or forty years later. He probably had the place to himself too.

I find myself wondering about that shower which hit Gray at the circle, since the same happened to me. I was soaked within minutes and it seemed like eternity as I walked as quickly as I could back down the hill. In fact, I got back to the town in half an hour and the rain stopped. I suspect Gray would have taken two or two and half hours on this little expedition and that it would have been six o'clock before he got back.

TAILPIECE: GRAY'S BOOKS CONVERSE

Mad: Sevigné. Mon cher Aristote! Do get a little further or you'll quite suffocate me.

Aristotle. [....] I have as much right to be here as you, and I shan't remove a jot.

M. Sevigné. Oh! The brute! Here's my poor Sixth Tome is squeezed to death: for God's sake, Bussy, come & rescue me.

Bussy Rabutin. Ma belle Cousine! I would fly to your assistance. Mais voici un Diable de Strabon qui me tue: I have nobody in my neighbourhood worth conversing with here but Catullus.

Bruyere. Patience! You must consider we are but books & so can't help ourselves. For my part, I wonder who we all belong to. We are a strange mixture here. I have a Malebranche on one Side of me, and a Gronovius on t'other.

Locke. Certainly our owner must have very confused ideas to jumble us so strangely together. He has associated me with Ovid & Ray the Naturalist.

[From a letter to West, December 1738]

Overleaf: Map of Broadwater, by James Clarke

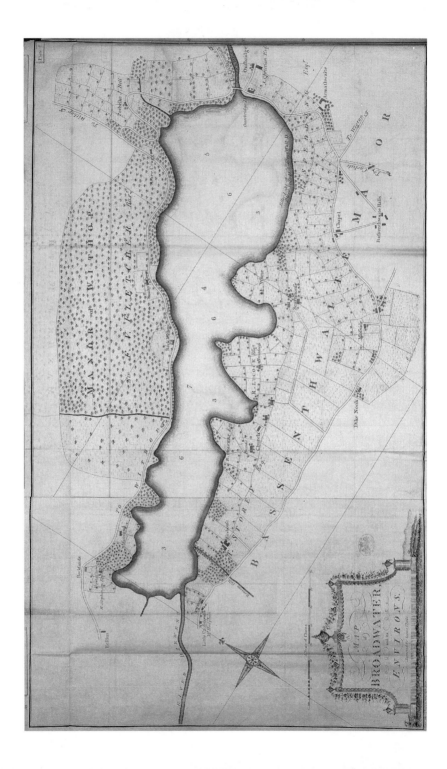

DAY SEVEN

The East Side of Bassenthwaite

Oct: 6. W^d E:, clouds & sun. went in a chaise 8 m. along the E. side of Bassinthwaite-water to Ews-bridge the road in some parts made, in others dangerous for a carriage, narrow, slippery & stony, but no precipices. it runs directly at the foot of Skiddaw, & opposite to Thornthwait-fells, & the brows of Widhope cover'd to the top with wood, opens a very beautiful view down the Lake, wch is narrower & longer than that of Keswick, less broke into bays & without islands. at the foot of it a few paces from the brink stands *Armathwait*, gently sloping upwards with a thick grove of Scotch firs round it, & a large wood behind it. it looks directly up the whole length of the lake almost to Keswick & beyond this a ridge of cultivated hills, on wch according to the Keswick-proverb the Sun always shines. [the inhabitants here on the contrary call the vale of Derwentwater *the Devil's Champerpot*, and pronounce the name of *Skiddaw-fell* (wch terminates here) with a sort of terror and aversion] a little to the west a stone bridge of 3 arches crosses the Derwent just where it issues from the lake & here I dined at an inn that stands there. *Armathwait* is a good modern house, not large, of dark-red stone, belonging to Mr Spedding, whose Gr:father was a Steward of old Sr James Lowther, & bought this estate of the *Himers*. so you must look for Mr Mitchell in some other country. the sky was overcast & the wind cool, so after sauntering a while by the water I came home again. a turnpike is brought from Cockermouth to Ews-bridge 5 miles & is carrying on to Penrith. several little showers to-day. said to be snow on *Cross-fell*.

COMMENTARY

JAMES Clarke, in his *Survey of the Lakes* (1789), attempted to explain the shortness of Gray's comments on this day in singular fashion. "When Mr Gray was at Keswick, he was desirous of seeing the back of Skiddaw, and accordingly took chaise to Ousebridge, thinking to have a view of the precipices by the way. Timidity, however, prevailed over curiosity so far, that he no sooner came within sight of those awful rocks than he put up the blinds of his carriage." In similar fashion, Clarke later accused Gray of refusing to venture on Windermere unless his eyes were blindfolded. Since Gray's itinerary did not give him time to go on the lake, it was obviously an invented story. Clarke himself described the road by Thirlmere as threatened "with large loose stones, which seem ready to drop from their sides on the smallest occasion; a sight of sufficient terror to hasten the traveller from a scene of such seemingly impending danger"; Gray describes *this* road as "very safe in broad daylight". On the whole, Clarke seems more alarmist and imaginative than Gray, though his story is typical of the denigration of Gray by the following generation of writers. The effect of that denigration is that what Gray writes is unjustly devalued by the falsely perceived personality behind the writing.

Clarke's map of Bassenthwaite, however, is useful in showing the route of the turnpike road to Cockermouth along the eastern shore of the lake and round by Armathwaite to Ousebridge, where there was then an inn, "a very good new building" [by Clarke's time] "erected purposely for travellers by the late Mr Spedding of Armathwaite". The road at that time ran close to the hall, which was a totally different building from the mansion built on the site by the Fletcher-Vane family in the nineteenth century and now transformed into a very up-market hotel. The Speddings moved out in 1796 to Mirehouse, further south down the lake, a fairly modest but pleasant house, still occupied by the Speddings. It is open to the public and is arguably one of the most rewarding small country-houses in the north to visit, because of its associations, its setting, and the warmth of its welcome.

Gray must have exchanged small talk at the "public house near the bridge" (as he refers to it) in order to get his pronunciation corrected and to pick up his story about the Devil's Chamberpot. The Devil has a Punchbowl, a Beeftub, a Bridge, a Dyke, and an Elbow elsewhere but a Chamberpot seems original. Perhaps there was a particularly imaginative local at the inn, inventing stories to please the neatly dressed stranger from London, since the proverb about the sun always shining at this end of the lake sounds like good local publicity too. The attitude towards Skiddaw, terror and aversion, is less easy to speculate about. Perhaps again it was invented to create the kind of aura that was thought to be pleasing to tourists - Clarke complains elsewhere of this kind of local exaggeration - but it may also be genuine. Skiddaw *is* fiercer and steeper on its northern flanks than on its benign southern face and there are still accidents on its ridges and crags. Gray seems to have spent some time pondering an ascent of Skiddaw but it would not have taken much of a hint of danger to put him off.

One later writer who did make the climb was Mrs Ann Radcliffe, author of *The Mysteries of Udolpho.* Her account of her expedition is usually quoted with the kind of condescension and ridicule unthinkingly considered to be justified by its different temper and outlook. If, however, it is read with an open mind, open to sensations no longer available to us but which must have been genuinely felt then, it may be seen as a beautifully written account, beautiful in detail and in spirit, as well as accurate.

> Having engaged a guide, and with horses accustomed to the labour, we began to ascend this tremendous mountain by a way which makes the summit five miles from Keswick.....
>
> At length as we ascended, Derwentwater dwindled on the eye to the smallness of a pond, while the grandeur of its amphitheatre was increased by new ranges of dark mountains, no longer individually great, but so from accumulation - a scenery to give ideas of the breaking up of a world. Other precipices soon hid it again; but Bassenthwaite continued to spread immediately below us, till we turned into the heart of Skiddaw and were enclosed by its steeps. We had now lost all track, even of the flocks that were spread over these tremendous wilds. The

guide conducted us by many curvings among the heathy hills and
hollows of the mountain; but the ascents were such that the horses
panted in the slowest walk and it was necessary to let them rest every
six or seven minutes. An opening to the south at length showed the
whole plan of the narrow vales of St John and Nadale, separated by the
dark ridge of rocks called St John's Rigg, with each its small line of
verdure at the bottom, and bounded by enormous grey fells, which we
were, however, now high enough to overlook.

Leaving this view, the mountain soon again shut off all
prospect but of its own valleys and precipices, covered with various
shades of turf and moss and with heath, of which a dull purple was the
prevailing hue. Not a tree nor bush appeared on Skiddaw, not even a
stone wall anywhere broke the simple greatness of its lines. Sometimes
we looked into tremendous chasms, where the torrent, heard roaring
long before it was seen, had worked itself a deep channel, and fell from
ledge to ledge, foaming and shining amidst the dark rock. These streams
are sublime, from the length and precipitancy of their course, which,
hurrying the sight with them into the abyss, act as it were in sympathy
with the nerves, and, to save ourselves from following, we recoil from
the view with involuntary horror. Of such, however, we saw only two,
and these by some departure from the usual course up the mountain; but
everywhere met gushing springs till we were within two miles of the
summit, when our guide added to the rum in his bottle what he said was
the last water we should find on our ascent.

The air now became very thin, and the steeps still more
difficult of ascent; but it was often delightful to look down into the
green hollows of the mountain, among pastoral scenes that wanted only
some mixture of wood to render them enchanting. About a mile from
the summit, the way was indeed dreadfully sublime, lying for nearly half
a mile along the edge of a precipice that passed with a swift descent, for
probably nearly a mile, into a glen within the heart of Skiddaw; and not
a bush nor a hillock interrupted its vast length, or, by offering a midway
check in the descent, diminished the fear it inspired. The ridgy steeps
of Saddleback formed the opposite boundary of the glen; and, though
really at a considerable distance, had, from the height of the two
mountains, such an appearance of nearness, that it almost seemed, as if

we could spring to its side. How much too did simplicity increase the sublimity of this scene, in which nothing but mountain, heath, and sky appeared! But our situation was too critical, or too unusual, to permit the just impressions of such sublimity. The hill rose so closely above the precipice as scarcely to allow a ledge wide enough for a single horse. We followed the guide in silence and, till we regained the more open wild, had no leisure for exclamation. After this, the ascent appeared easy, and we were bold enough to wonder that the steeps near the beginning of the mountain had excited any anxiety.

At length, passing the skirts of the two points of Skiddaw which are nearest to Derwentwater, we approached the third and loftiest and then perceived that their steep sides, together with the ridges that connect them, were entirely covered near their summits with a whitish shivered slate, which threatens to slide down with every gust of wind. The broken state of this slate makes the present summits seem like the ruins of others - a circumstance as extraordinary in appearance as difficult to be accounted for.

The ridge on which we passed from the neighbourhood of the second summit to the third was narrow, and the eye reached, on each side, down the whole extent of the mountain, following on the left the rocky precipices that impend over the lake of Bassenthwaite and looking on the right into the glens of Saddleback, far, far, below. But the prospects that burst upon us from every part of the vast horizon, when we had gained the summit, were such as we had scarcely dared to hope for and must now rather venture to enumerate than to describe....

The air on this summit was boisterous, intensely cold, and difficult to be inspired, though below the day was warm and serene. It was dreadful to look down from nearly the brink of the point on which we stood upon the lake of Bassenthwaite, and over a sharp and separated ridge of rocks that from below appeared of tremendous height, but now seemed not to reach half way up Skiddaw....

We reached Keswick about four o'clock, after five hours passed in this excursion, in which the care of our guide greatly lessened the notion of danger.

Gray had had a chance to go up Skiddaw three days before but he had decided to go down Borrowdale instead, perhaps because of his inability to ride or because he needed a companion to urge him on, but he remained worried by it. Skiddaw's commanding presence and height and its ease of ascent must have given it an early reputation, which lingers on, even if Helvellyn has probably replaced it in primacy of popularity. It is clearly important to repeat that eighteenth-century pilgrimage, if one is to regain anything of the age's feel for landscape, but there are problems. The most interestingly varied routes of ascent are from the north, up the ridge over Ullock Pike or from the waterfall at Dash Beck, but they do not give the relationship to Keswick. The original tourist path from the south is an excellent route, both for views on the way up or down and for ease of gradient, but it has one serious drawback: it is heavily used by large groups of visitors between the hours of 10 and 6, particularly at summer weekends. It is essential, if one is to enjoy the peace and beauty and grandeur of the mountain, either to make an alpine start (i.e. at about 5 or 6 a.m.), or to go up in the evening, or, better still, to go up in moonlight; that means on the night of a full, or nearly full, moon, rising soon after it is dusk. Wainwright, who knew these fells better than most, specifically recommends Skiddaw "for a night climb, preferably with the help of a moon". Not only does one get the mountain to oneself but one also sees it in unusual lights and shadows which may recapture that early sense of awe and excitement.

One should start from the bottom by the track that goes across the footbridge over the A66 and contours round Latrigg. There is, however, a car-park at the top of Gale Road, to the north of Latrigg, and this has the advantages, for a moonlight ascent, of starting 1000 feet up on the open mountainside and of not disturbing the good citizens of Keswick at an unearthly hour. I started at 2 a.m. one June night two days after a full moon. The moon was concealed by wispy cloud at first and I needed a head-torch for the first half-mile between two fences to the foot of the first real incline. We are not naturally night creatures and it takes time to develop an obstacle sense and a feel for the dark masses all round and the gloomy light. It all reminded me of my training as a National Serviceman when we were told on a night exercise never to look at a source of light but to keep our heads down - and I missed the flare that was fired to end the exercise. On this night the moonlight strengthened and the cloud cleared and the moon climbed to its zenith. After half an hour it was throwing a faint shadow on the ground in front of me and I had no further need of the torch. One of the beauties of the darkness was that one could not see the steepness of the ascent and so one climbed steadily without thinking of it or feeling the pain. The odd plane-light went on and off in the sky; a lighthouse on the Scottish side of the Solway flashed at regular intervals; patterns of sodium lights showed the extent of Keswick below and of Whitehaven and Workington to the west, even, as one got higher, of Ambleside to the south. One straight stretch of the A66 showed up like an airport runway. The eighteenth century could not compete with the scale of this extravagant illumination and indeed it can be seen as a form of pollution. In more relaxed mood one can just enjoy the intricate patterns.

The path climbs the slopes of Jenkin Hill, crosses behind Low Man, and climbs again to the South Top from which one walks over the summit plateau to the true North Top - the same route as Radcliffe's, although it may not easily be recognizable as such. It was half past three when I got there. There was a streak of light along the eastern horizon. A cold wind was blowing. Wainwright, to his recommendation, adds a warning that, "The summit of Skiddaw can be Arctic even on a night in midsummer". As (almost) always, he was right. It reminded me of another night visit to the top of Skiddaw on the Queen's Jubilee in June 1977, when it had snowed and the wind had blown the flames of the beacon bonfire horizontally in great gusts. Despite the cold, it was a superb feeling, being above the dim shapes of all the great hills, with the lakes of Derwentwater and Bassenthwaite showing up lighter below, but better was to come. I made my way down after twenty minutes on the top, leaving the tourist path to visit the top of Low Man. The eastern light was now tinged with red below a grey cloud bank and I realized the sunrise was not far off. At 4.32 a red rim appeared, firing the undersides of the clouds with a shaft of red light. It took six wonderful minutes for the red disk fully to reveal itself, the red spreading further out under the clouds across to the west, finally touching the tops of Scafell and Pillar and Gable with a rosy glow. By the end I could hardly see for tears of amazement or exhilaration (or perhaps it was just the wind in my eyes). Yet the sun presumably puts on more or less the same performance every day. Gray had a similar experience of the sunrise, but some years before on the south coast.

> I set out one morning before 5 o'clock, the moon shining through a dark and misty autumnal air, and got to the sea-coast time enough to be at the Sun's Levee. I saw the clouds and dark vapour open gradually to right and left, rolling over one another in great smoky wreathes; and the tide (as it flowed in gently upon the sands) first whitening, then gently tinged with gold and blue: and all at once a little line of insufferable brightness that (before I can write these five words) was grown to half an orb, and now to a whole one, too glorious to be distinctly seen. It is very odd it makes no figure on paper; yet I shall remember it as long as the sun, or at least as long as I endure. I wonder whether any body saw it before? I hardly believe it [19 Nov. 1764].

I felt the same unforgettable experience as Gray but it was Coleridge I thought of at the time, walking from Greta Hall below across to the Helvellyn hills and along the tops to visit Wordsworth. They too had experienced this kind of epiphany, this manifestation of an uncanny beauty, at various times, in natural displays, rainbows, moonlight, freak winds.

To my surprise, three people were coming up; half an hour later I met two more, and then another. This is the way to see this hill and a few people seem to know it. I was down by 6 and back in bed by 7.30, waking jet-lagged an hour later. It is a small price to pay and it only takes a firm decision (or a determined wife's encouragement in my case) to make you do it.

Gray's mention of snow on Cross Fell is his fourth mention of this hill, which clearly had an important place in his scheme of reference. Its status as a mountain was much higher in the eighteenth century than it is now. It was thought to be the highest mountain in England, over three thousand feet high, and to have permanent snow. It was indeed a mountain then, not just high moorland, as it tends to be thought of now. At that time all high ground was seen as mountainous and George Smith devoted an article in *The Gentleman's Magazine* to a visit to "Cross Fell Mountain". Part of the change that has happened is that we now make different distinctions and look for shape as well as height in our mountains. Snow helps to make them wild and inaccessible and there was more snow in the Little Ice Age, that extended at least to the end of the eighteenth century. Even now, however, there is snow recorded on Cross Fell for long periods of time, on 105 days of the year in 1973, and there were patches of snow remaining on the north side of the summit well into June of 1995, as we could see from our house in Carlisle.

TAILPIECE:THE TRAVELS OF T: G: GENT: which will consist of the following particulars:

Chap. 11

Sets out the latter end of November to cross the Alps. He is devoured by a wolf, & how it is to be devoured by a Wolf. The 7th day he comes to the foot of Mount Cenis. How he is wrapp'd up in Bear Skins, & Beaver Skins, Boots on his legs, Muffs on his hands, & Taffety over his eyes; he is placed on a Bier, & is carried to heaven by the savages blindfold. How he lights among a certain fat nation call'd Clouds, how they are always in a Sweat, & never speak, but they fart. How they flock about him, & think him very odd for not doing so too. He falls flump into Italy.

[from a letter to Dr Wharton, March, 1740]

Overleaf: Map of Derwentwater by James Clarke

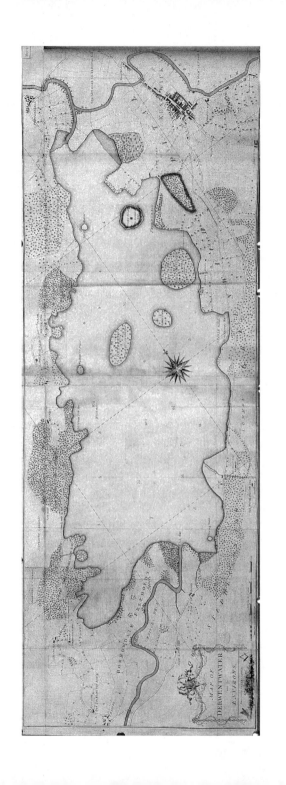

DAY EIGHT

Crow Park and the Penrith Road

Oct:7. market day here. Wd N:E: clouds & sun. little showers at intervals all day. yet walk'd in the morning to Crow-park, & in the evening up Penrith-road. the clouds came rolling up the mountains all round very unpromising; yet the moon shone at intervals. it was too damp to go towards the lake. tomorrow mean to bid farewell to Keswick.

Botany might be studied here in perfection at another season because of the great variety of situations & soils all lieing within a small compass. I observed nothing but several curious sorts of Lichens, & plenty of gale (*Myrica Gale*) or Dutch myrtle, perfuming the borders of the lake. this year the *Wadd mine* has been open'd (wch is done once in 5 Years. it is taken out sometimes in lumps as big as a man's fist, & will undergo no preparation by fire, not being fusible. when it is pure, soft, black, & close-grain'd, it is worth sometimes 30 shillings a pound. the mine lies about a mile up the Fells, near *See-wait* at the head of Borrodale.

There are no Charr ever taken in these waters, but many in Butter-mere-water about Martinmas, wch are brought hither & potted. They sow chiefly oats & bigg here, wch is but now cutt, & still on the ground. there is some hay not yet got in. the rains have done much hurt. [yet observe, the soil is so thin & light, that no day has pass'd, in wch I could not walk out with ease, & you know, I am no lover of dirt]. their wheat comes from Cockermouth or Penrith. Fell-mutton is now in season. it grows fat on the mountains, & much resembles venison: excellent Perch (here called *Bass*)& Pike; & partridge in plenty.

Receipt to dress Perch (for Mrs Wharton)

Wash, but neither scale, nor gut them. broil till they are enough; then pull out the fins, & open them along ye back, take out the bone & all the inwards without breaking them. put in a large lump of butter & salt, clap the sides together, till it melts, & serve very hot. it is excellent. the skin must not be eaten.

COMMENTARY

THIS was the nearest thing that Gray experienced to a rainy day and perhaps he was beginning to run out of things to do. He didn't want to do the touristy trips, like going on the lake or up the mountain, and he had seen what he had wanted to see. There was, however, no pressure of time. This Cambridge professor did not have to hurry back to the university for the beginning of term, and, if he carried a watch, he seems rarely to have consulted it, for there are few mentions of exact time in this journal. What controls Gray's day is the weather ("too damp") and the availability of light ("the moon shone"). Crow Park was established as a morning station because the light filled the valley; Crosthwaite Vicarage became an evening station because of the sunset effects to the west. There is a leisurely attitude towards time by modern standards, and yet this was an age that was becoming increasingly interested in time. An accurate clock gradually became a necessity; factory shift times were introduced; stage coaches raced against time. Edward Young, who wrote one of the longest poems in the English language, might have good reason to boast that "we take no note of time", but he also knew, famously, that "Procrastination is the thief of time". The sales of calendars, almanacs, and notebooks for diaries soared; the printer, Robert Dodsley, pioneered a highly successful *Memorandum Book*, a fore-runner of the modern filofax. Gray, however, was content with an old notebook; he was not keeping a diary. Fortuitously he had discovered for himself a new literary hybrid, a journal which was also a series of letters. Consciously or unconsciously, he followed Defoe's advice to take "some Minutes of Things for his own satisfaction...very critical[....] and upon some very significant things". He did not try to give a full account of every day. It did make a difference worth noticing by Gray that it was market day. The fact that that was (and still is) a Saturday was, however, of no special significance, for Saturday does not seem to have been a special day. The touch of mock-heroic in the remark, "mean to bid farewell to Keswick", seems to suggest Gray's consciousness of coming to the end of a memorable experience, life-changing in a way that is now difficult to appreciate. He had made time enough.

Gray was a botanist of some skill and experience. His note-books and letters both contain regular and detailed meteorological and botanical observations and he corresponded with leading observers of his day, with Thomas Pennant, Gilbert White, and with the Swedish scientist, Linnaeus. He had an extensive and up-to-date library of the most comprehensive kind, which he annotated: Buffon, Linnaeus, and Hudson's recently published *Flora Anglica*. Carlisle Public Library has a copy of this last work with the words, "The notes in this book were wrote by the celebrated Mr Gray the poet". There is evidence of more than one hand in the marginalia and no convincing evidence from place or personal names that the notes are by Gray. There is, however, a recipe inside the fly-leaf, which looks like the kind of thing Gray collected, and the tone of some of the observations, as well as the smallness and regularity of some of the handwriting, with the occasional note in Latin or Greek, make it possible that at least some of the notes are by Gray. In a marginal addition about angelica, for example, the writer notes that it has "white flowers purplish white the leaves blacker and narrower than garden angel [....] smell nearly the same". That sounds like Gray. Bog myrtle can apparently still be found on the shores of Derwentwater. I have never personally found it but it is recorded in the modern *Flora of Cumbria* near Nicol End and at the south-west foot of the lake. It must have suffered from grazing or drainage, for the National Trust is attempting to fence off some parts of the shoreline to enable the fenland habitat to recover. In his note-book for his 1767 visit Gray records that he saw at Keswick *Sorbus aucuparia* (rowan), *Sedum telephium* (orpine), *Lythrum salicaria* (purple loosestrife), and *Campanula trachelium* (nettle-leaved bell-flower). Of these, the last appears now to be very rare.

One book that we know that Gray possessed is *A Complete System of Cookery* by William Verral, published in 1759, since the copy, with Gray's annotations, is in the Rare Books section of the British Library. In the front and rear blank pages, Gray has written in a large number of recipes, how to dress an eel or a carp or loaches or dace or pike: he seems to have been particularly fond of fish. It should be no surprise, therefore, that in this journal entry he should insert a recipe for Mrs Wharton. Some writers on Gray paint a picture of him effeminately breakfasting on apricot marmalade. It becomes a different picture when you realize that he probably made his own marmalade and cooked many of his own meals: it may or may not be manly to be interested in cookery but it does show strong individuality. It is not surprising either that Gray should have been interested in potted charr. Charr is a deepwater fish, not very large, caught on special rod and line set-ups. They are still caught in Buttermere, as in Gray's day, though it has disappeared from Ullswater owing to pollution. It was probably a delicacy then, with a taste like salmon, but it seems to be unobtainable now, even at Fortnum and Masons.

Gray is less reliable on the value of the wadd (i.e. graphite), which he seems to have considerably over-priced. Apparently the price could vary from 8 to 17 shillings a pound according to quality. In 1760 the mine was opened and seven tons were extracted, valued at £3,000. Such a sum, however, was a small fortune then, since one has to multiply by 60 or 80 to obtain a modern equivalent. Theft on a large scale was, not surprisingly, a problem. The mine was attacked by an organized gang in 1768 and a considerable quantity of wad stolen, some of which was later recovered from a secret hiding place high in the fells. The lead was used for medicinal and industrial purposes but not yet in "pencils". That industry, for which Keswick became famous, came later in the early 1800s. The word "pencil" in Gray's time still usually referred to a paintbrush. Curiously, it does not seem to have occurred to Gray that a mining operation might deface or spoil an area of natural beauty. It was another of the attractions of the area to him, a matter of interest to any gentleman with a scientific turn of mind. "Fusible" is a nice specimen of eighteenth-century scientific jargon and is a sure sign of Gray's gentlemanly interest in all aspects of natural history and natural science. These were the days of amateur experimentation, when Dr Brownrigg of Keswick, aided and abetted by Benjamin Franklin, emptied several gallons of oil into Derwentwater to test the placating effects on stormy water.

The admission by Gray that he was "no lover of the dirt" is another revealing phrase. Its ironic understatement makes clear Gray's delicacy: he would not, one presumes, like to get sweaty or soaked to the skin or to appear scruffy or dirty. He must have been finicky about his shirts and stockings and cravats and shoes. It is not surprising that he did not ride or depart from safe paths or go out in a boat.

TAILPIECE: TWO MORE GRAY RECIPES.

Oxford Pudding: Take grated bread, shred suet, pick'd currants, sugar, of each a quarter of a pound, mix together; grate in a good deal of lemon-peel & nutmeg, break in two eggs, stir all together, tie in a fine cloth & boil ½ an hour or more.

Sauce for Steaks: A glass of Ale, 2 anchovies, a little thyme, savoury, parsley, nutmeg, & lemon-peel shred altogether. When the steaks are ready pour out the liquor & put the Ale &c. into the pan with some butter roll'd in flower & when hot, strain it over the Steaks. Have a care the Ale is not bitter.

[From Gray's copy of Wm. Verral's A Complete System of Cookery]

Overleaf: Grasmere, by Joseph Farington

DAY NINE

Keswick to Kendal by Grasmere

Oct: 8. Bid farewell to *Keswick* & took the *Ambleside* road in a gloomy morning. W^d. E: & afterwards N: E:. about 2 m: from the town mounted an eminence called *Castle-rig*, & the sun breaking out discover'd the most beautiful [enchanting] view I have yet seen of the whole valley behind me, the two lakes, the river, & all the mountains [all in their glory]. had almost a mind to have gone back again.

The road in some little patches is not compleated yet, but good country road thro' a few narrow & stony lanes, very safe in broad daylight. this is the case about *Causeway-foot* & among *Naddle*-Fells to *Lainwaite* [Legburthwaite]. the vale you go in has little breadth, the mountains are vast & rocky, the fields little & poor, & the inhabitants are now making hay, [&] see not the sun by two hours in a day so long as at Keswick.

Came to the foot of *Helvellyn* along wch an excellent road is carried, looking down from a little height on Lee's-water (call'd also *Thirl-meer*, or *Wiborn-water*) & soon descending on its margin. the water looks black from its depth (tho' really clear as glass) & from the gloom of the vast crags, that scowl over it: it is narrow & about 3 m: long, resembling a river in its course. little shining torrents hurry down the rocks to join it, but not a bush to overshadow them, or cover their march. all is rock & loose stones up to the very brow, wch lies so near your way, that not above half the height of Helvellyn can be seen.

Past by the little Chappel of Wiborn, out of wch the Sunday-congregation were then issuing.

Past a beck near *Dunmail-raise*, & enter'd *Westmoreland* a second time. now begin to see *Helm-Crag* distinguish'd from its rugged neighbours not so much by its height, as by the strange broken outline of its top, like some gigantic building demolish'd, & the stones that composed it, flung cross each other in wild confusion. just beyond it opens one of the sweetest landscapes, that art ever attempted to imitate. (the bosom of ye mountains spreading here into a broad bason) discovers in the midst Grasmere-water. its margin is hollow'd into small bays with bold eminences some of rock, some of soft turf, that half conceal, & vary the figure [of] the little lake they command, from the shore a low promontory pushes itself far into the water, & on it stands a white village with the parish-church rising in the midst of it, hanging enclosures, corn-fields, & meadows green as an emerald with their trees & hedges & cattle fill up the whole space from the edge of the water & just opposite to you is a large farmhouse at the bottom of a steep smooth lawn embosom'd in old woods, wch climb half-way up the mountain's side, & discover above them a broken line of crags, that crown the scene. not a single red tile, no flaring Gentleman's house, or garden-walls, break in upon the repose of this little unsuspected paradise, but all is peace, rusticity, & happy poverty in its neatest most becoming attire.

The road winds here over *Grasmere*-hill, whose rocks soon conceal the water from your sight, yet it is continued along behind them, & contracting itself to a river communicates with Ridale-water, another small lake, but of inferior size & beauty. it seems shallow too, for large patches of reeds appear pretty far within it. into this vale the road descends. on the opposite banks large & ancient woods mount up the hills, & just to the left of our way stands *Rydale*-hall, the family seat of Sr Mic: Fleming, but now a farm-house, a large old-fashion'd fabrick surrounded with wood & not much too good for its present destination. Sr Michael is now on his travels, & all this timber far & wide belongs to him. I tremble for it, when he returns. near the house rises a huge crag call'd *Rydale-head*, wch is said to command a full view of Wynander-mere, & I doubt it not, for within a mile that great Lake is visible even from the road. as to going up the crag one might as well go up Skiddaw.

Came to Ambleside, 18 m: from Keswick meaning to lie there, but on looking into the best bed-chamber dark & damp as a cellar grew delicate, gave up Wynander-mere in despair & resolved I would go on to Kendal directly, 14 m: farther. the road in general fine turnpike, but some parts (about 3 m: in all) not made, yet without danger.

Unexpectedly was well-rewarded for my determination. the

afternoon was fine, & the road for full 5 m: runs along the side of Windermere with delicious views across it & almost from one end to the other. it is ten miles in length, & at most a mile over, resembling the course of some vast & magnificent river, but no flat marshy grounds, no osier-beds, or patches of scrubby plantation on its banks. at the head two vallies open among the mountains, one that by wch we came down, the other *Langsledale* [Langdale] in w^{ch} *Wreenose* [Wrynose] & *Hardknott*, two great mountains, rise above the rest. from thence the fells visibly sink & soften along its sides, sometimes they run into it (but with a gentle declivity) in their own dark & natural complexion, oftener they are green & cultivated with farms interspersed & round eminences on the border cover'd with trees: towards the South it seem'd to break into larger bays with several islands & a wider extent of cultivation. the way rises continually till at a place call'd *Orrest-head* it turns to S:E: losing sight of the water.

Pass'd by *Ings-Chappel*, & *Staveley*, but I can say no farther, for the dusk of evening coming on I enter'd *Kendal* almost in the dark, & could distinguish only a shadow of the Castle on a hill & tenter-grounds spread far and wide round the Town, wch I mistook for houses. my inn promised sadly having two wooden galleries (like Scotland) in front of it. it was indeed an old ill-contrived house but kept by civil sensible people, so I stay'd two nights with them & fared & slept very comfortably.

COMMENTARY

THIS is another road which has altered in width and surface and route, not only since Gray but also since the days when Wordsworth's Waggoner rolled along it. The road then climbed steeply out of Keswick to a brow, at which it may well have been necessary as well as desirable to stop for a look at "the most beautiful view"; to do so now causes a major traffic hazard. The road then became a narrow, walled, stony lane, twisting its way over hummocky ground; now it is a broad sweep of high-speed asphalt. The major difference, however, is beyond Thirlspot as a result of the flooding in the 1880s by Manchester Corporation of the original small lake, then called variously Leathes Water (after a local landowner) or Wyborn-water or Thirlmere. That lake was in two halves, bridged at its narrowest point south of Dale Head, and there was a sizable settlement at its head at Wythburn, one group of houses ironically named on early maps as the "City". The road which followed its shoreline is now under water, as are various groups of houses and farms and two inns, one the Nag's Head, where Keats had trouble with the fleas in 1818, the other, the Cherry Tree, where Wordsworth's Waggoner succumbed to the demon drink. Conifer plantations shroud both sides of the road; the water in the "little shining torrents" is now tapped off into a buried aqueduct and the lake, "clear as glass", is dark and the shore tide-marked by dropping water-levels; the hillsides are scarred white with broad eroded footpaths to Helvellyn's magnetic summit; and the lake itself is four, rather than three, miles long from head to dam. This is now a dismal and uninteresting road on which to travel; the narrow lane on the western shore is far pleasanter, if you have the time, or you can also find peace at Dale Head Hall, now by-passed by the new road.

It comes as a mild surprise to find Gray travelling on this road on a Sunday, in view of the moral opprobrium cast on Sunday travelling in Jane Austen's *Persuasion*; Gray seems to have had no qualms about setting off home on a Sunday nor does he seem to be conscious that perhaps he should have joined the little congregation at Wythburn that he met coming out, though it is clear from his letters and writing that he was a sincere Christian. He might well, of course, have thought the little chapel a rather mean and uninviting building, since in essence it is like a long, low farm building with simple windows and a bare raftered roof inside. It has had a pleasant apse added to its east end some time in the nineteenth century to give it a little more dignity and it now seems to have a Quakerly simplicity. Services are still held regularly, though its local community has all but disappeared. The following note inside the church (1998) may give some indication of its present fortunes.

> In July last year some of the slates were stolen from this church
> roof, and everything was in turmoil, as you can imagine. The church

was open to the elements for several weeks, but the Church Council and friends have taken the opportunity to re-roof the building in the traditional manner. The church has been re-decorated and we have cleaned it to the best of our ability. This has still not prevented further attacks (e.g. the wall safe) but we are determined to keep this lovely and historic church open to the public for prayers or just to enjoy.

William Gilpin expected banditti a little further along the road, on Dunmail Raise. "Of all the scenes I ever saw, this was the most adapted to the perpetration of some dreadful deed. The imagination can hardly avoid conceiving a band of robbers lurking under the shelter of some projecting rock." One or two destitutes or outlaws would have made a Picturesque addition to the scene. This now seems one of the easiest and least dramatic passes in the district.

It is not surprising that Helm Crag should catch Gray's eye from the top of Dunmail Raise. Its summit is, as he says, a "wild confusion of rocks" giving "a strange broken outline" to its low but commanding summit. "Like some gigantic building demolished", is Gray's parallel but it is also sometimes known as The Lion and the Lamb or as The Lady and the Piano or even as The Howitzer. Wordsworth referred to it as The Astrologer at his Desk. Closer acquaintance bears out this impression of ruggedness, for it is one of the few Lakeland tops that it is very difficult to reach without a slightly scary scramble. There is no way that Gray would have climbed this one. "One might as well as go up Skiddaw," as he says of Nab Scar (Rydale Head): all are equally impossible.

Gray's description of Grasmere as a "little unsuspected paradise" [where] "all is peace, rusticity, and happy poverty" - an afterthought in the original journal, written in over the top of the line - epitomizes a widely held attitude towards country-life, an attitude which can, at first sight, be sharply criticized. It can be argued, of course, that it enshrines the artificiality of the urban, escapist idealization of rural poverty, an attitude, which persists in the prettification of the rustic cottage, of agricultural pursuits and customs, and of a dehumanized landscape. This is a popular attitude, persisting in calendars and postcards and certain kinds of travel-writing and film-making, popular because the peace and happiness which it conveys are earnestly desired by people whose ordinary lives have little enough of either. It can be criticized as an untruth, as a misinterpretation of what is really happening in the countryside. It is easy to see Gray's phrase, "happy poverty", as complacent and tolerant of social inequality, as *The Elegy Written in a Country Churchyard* also appears to be, if you read it as William Empson read it. Yet there is an element of truth in Gray's idea, even if some of Wordsworth's poems, like *The Ruined Cottage* or *Michael*, give a less attractive view of rural poverty. There is such a thing as contentment with simplicity and the poor may in that sense be blessed, even if few people in practice ever are so contented. Gray's idea is a powerful one: it is an idea which still motivates many to escape from the town to a simpler life in natural surroundings. The young William Wilberforce saw Grasmere as the original of Rasselas's Happy Valley. Perhaps it was some such utopian concept, or the direct influence of Gray's words, that led Wordsworth to choose Dove Cottage as his poetic environment - or perhaps it was just that the rent was right.

When Gray moves on to the supposedly "inferior" Rydal, he makes some curious remarks about the trees round Sir Michael Fleming's family seat at Rydal Hall. The wood is "not much too good for its present destination" and he "trembles" for the timber. Because the young aristocrat from Rydal Hall was away on his Grand Tour, Gray assumes he must be a young tearaway and that the felling of trees was the kind of vandalism to be expected of a more general loose living. Perhaps Gray was lucky to find him out, since thirty years later an older and more reactionary Sir Michael sent his servant to reprimand Coleridge, when he had the temerity to walk in front of the house. By Coleridge's day, Sir Michael had also had the house painted fashionably white: "damned whitewashing" in Coleridge's eyes, and probably in Gray's too, since it was this aristocratic fashion that made gentlemen's houses "flaring."

Ambleside was a much smaller town then than Keswick or Kendal and its main inn, the Salutation probably, not yet used to tourist demands, may well have been damp and dreary. Gray seems to blame himself for being over-delicate but we have all turned away from unprepossessing places in a state of indecision and it is worth remembering the hazards of eighteenth-century inns. James Ward, on a sketching tour thirty years or so later, records returning to "filthy food, black cabbage soup out of a common bowl, bad eggs, salt fish, underbaked oatcakes, stinking ham, butter full of cow hairs, gravy compacted with coal dust, and then a bed that was dirty, damp, and running with bugs"! Gray did appreciate the inn at Kendal with its "civil and sensible people" and the good fare and the good nights' rest he got there, though he did miss some interesting country as a result of pressing on. Gray, of course, was not to know that he was leaving the Lake District, since there was no tourist area with defined borders yet. The shape of Gray's tour is thus different from what we expect and yet it left a pattern - Ullswater, Keswick, Grasmere, Windermere - that other visitors followed for a considerable period of time.

TAILPIECE: GRAY ON TURNPIKES

At Keswick learnt, that the turn-pike road from thence along the east side of Bassinthwaite, or Low-water (which is eight miles) is made in part only, about three miles of it being a cart-road slippery and dangerous, or else narrow and stony lane. The new road from Cockermouth is made (five miles) to Ews-bridge, and now carrying on towards Penrith. That the way from Keswick to Ambleside (eighteen miles) is turnpike not yet compleated by about three miles. The unmade way is thro' narrow country lanes or rocky road, but nothing dangerous by daylight. It runs mostly thro' deep romantic vallies by the waters of Wiborn at the foot of Helvellin-fell, by Grasmere and Ridall. Amble-side is a little market-town, but the inns are too mean and unfrequented to lie at. From thence to Kendal is fourteen miles, turnpike road, but not quite finish'd; it goes near five miles on the side of Winander-water with beautiful views, mostly up-hill, but good road, except a small part not yet compleated & this is very safe...

[From a note in the first of the Murray Notebooks]

Overleaf: Kendal Castle, by Samuel and Nathaniel Buck

THE EAST VIEW OF KENDAL-CASTLE, IN THE COUNTY OF WESTMORLAND.

AT what Time, or by Whom, this Castle was built, we can not find in History, but it may be presum'd that it was the Manſion of the ancient Barons of Kendal, the firſt of which was Ivo Taileboys, of whose Posterity William, by consent of Henry II. call'd himself William of Lancaster. ——— 1. Kendal Town.

Sam.le & Nath.l Buck delin. Sculp. Publish'd according to the y.e Parliament. March 20. 1739.

DAY TEN

Kendal & Sizergh

Oct: 9. W^d N:W: clouds & sun. air mild as summer. all corn off the ground, sky-larks singing aloud (by the way I saw not one at Keswick, perhaps because the place abounds in birds of prey). went up the Castle-hill. the Town consists chiefly of three nearly parallel streets almost a mile long. except these all the other houses seem as if they had been dancing a country-dance & were out: there they stand back to back, corner to corner, some up hill, some down without intent or meaning. along by their side runs a fine brisk stream, over wch are 3 stone-bridges. the buildings (a few comfortable houses excepted) are mean, of stone & cover'd with a bad rough-cast. near the end of the town stands a handsome house of Col: Wilson's, & adjoining to it the Church, a very large Gothick fabrick with a square Tower. it has no particular ornaments but double isles, & at the east-end 4 chappels, or choirs. one of the *Pars*, another of the *Stricklands*, the 3^d is the proper choir of ye church, & the 4th of y^e *Bellingcams*, a family now extinct. there is an altar-tomb of one of them dated 1577 with a flat brass, arms & quarterings. & in the window their arms alone, Arg: a hunting-horn, sab: strung Gules. in the *Strickland's* chappel several modern monuments, & another old altar- tomb, not belonging to the family: on the side of it, a Fess dancetty between 10 Billets (Deincourt?). in the *Parr*-chappel is a third altar-tomb in the corner, no fig: or inscription, but on the side cut in stone an escutcheon of *Roos* of Kendal (3 Water-Budgets) quartering *Parr* (2 bars in a bordure engrail'd). 2dly an escutcheon, Vaire, a Fess (for Marmion). 3dly. an escutcheon. three Chevronels braced & a Chief (wch I take for Fitzhugh) at the foot is an escutcheon surrounded with the Garter, bearing *Roos* & *Parr* quarterly, quartering the other two beforemention'd. I have no books to look in, therefore can not say. Whether this the Ld *Parr of Kendal* (Queen Catherine's Father) or her Brother, the Marquis of *Northampton*. it is a Cenotaph for the latter, who was buried at Warwick in 1571. the remains of the Castle are seated on a fine hill on the side of the river opposite to the town. almost the whole enclosure of the walls remains with 4 towers, 2 square & 2 or 3 round, but their upper part & embattlements are demolished. it is of rough stone & cement, without any ornament or arms, round enclosing a court of like form & surrounded by a mote, nor ever could have been larger than it is, for there are no traces of outworks. there is a good view of the town & river with fertile open valley, thro' wch it winds.

After dinner went along the Milthrop-turnpike 4 m: to see the falls (or force) of the river *Kent*. Came to *Siserge* (pronounce Siser) & turn'd down a lane to the left. Siser, the seat of the *Stricklands* an old Catholick family, is an ancient Hall-house, with a very large tower embattled: the rest of the buildings added to this are of later date, but all is white & seen to advantage on a back ground of old trees: there is a small park also well-wooded. opposite to this turn'd to the left & soon came to the river. it works its way in a narrow & deep rocky channel o'erhung with trees. the calmness & brightness of ye evening, the roar of the waters, & the thumping of huge hammers at an iron-forge not far distant made it a singular walk, but as to the falls (for there are two) they are not 4 feet high. I went on down to the forge & saw the Dæmons at work by the light of their own fires: the iron is brought in pigs to Milthrop by sea from Scotland &c. & is here beat into bars & plates. two miles farther at *Levens* is the seat of Ld Suffolk, where he sometimes passes the summer. it was a favourite place of his late Countess: but this I did not see.

COMMENTARY

KENDAL has had a struggle to preserve its character from the car and the developer and, though a good number of eighteenth-century houses survive, the basically simple pattern of its streets is less easy to see now. There are indeed only three main streets - Highgate, Stricklandgate and Stramongate - but they are not "parallel" to one another, as Gray wrongly remembers. It is uncharacteristic of Gray to make such a mistake, as he was a believer in there-and-then writing: "Half a word fixed upon or near the spot, is worth a cart-load of recollection," he told his friend Palgrave [6 Sept. 1758]. Stricklandgate is, in fact, a continuation of Highgate, making one very long street - nearly a mile long, as Gray here rightly says - and Stramongate runs down from it and over the river. The main streets had, and still have in part, yards running off them, up the fellside or down to the river. These houses were indeed "mean" and closely packed and unhygienically drained by ginnels and some would be at odds with others, "as if they had been dancing a country dance". Down by the river and on an island in the river there were at that time extensive tenter-grounds for the drying of cloth. Tenters were fences about four and a half feet high, up to two hundred yards in length and parallel to each other. They have been compared more romantically to espaliered vines in a vineyard but they might also look like terraced houses in the dusk. The common phrase comparing suspense to being "on tenterhooks" seems to originate with the novelist Smollett at about this time. Some of the old inns, such as The [Golden] Fleece, dating from 1654, still survive, but the White Lion, where apparently Gray stayed, with its even-then old-fashioned galleried front, disappeared in the last century. It is a curious coincidence that the White Lion was also the birthplace of William Hudson, the botanist, whose *Flora Anglica* Gray often consulted. One of Kendal's more curious attractions at the time, at least for Thomas West, was its "workhouse for the poor, which for neatness and oeconomy exceeds most of the kind in the kingdom". The handsome house of Colonel Wilson that Gray mentions had not long been built. It is now known as Abbot Hall, being sited on land originally belonging to St Mary's Abbey at York, and is now an exceptionally fine art gallery. The church with its grand square tower is close by and is indeed very large, like an East Anglian wool church and financed by the same profits. It is alleged that the entire population of the town, which might have been about 2,000 when it was built (c.1540), could have been accommodated inside it. Gray made another mistake in counting the number of "chapels", since it has five, not four.

Gray seems to have missed some other things, such as the memorial to a Jacobean vicar, which begins intriguingly:

London bredd me, Westminster fedd me,
Cambridge sped me, my sister wed me....

The vicar may not have been admitting to incest: perhaps he meant that his sister arranged his marriage, or that he got married at his sister university of Oxford, or perhaps he just meant that his sister was as good as a wife in looking after him in his celibacy. What clearly did fascinate Gray, however, was the heraldry on the tombs and windows and his knowledge of heraldic detail is impressive; his *Commonplace Book* has sixty pages of notes on heraldry. A "fess" is a broad horizontal band crossing the escutcheon or shield in the centre and, if it is "dancetté", it is zigzagged. A "bordure engrail'd" was a border with scooped or scalloped edges and was a common mark of bastardy. A "chevronel" is a diminutive of "chevron", that is, of an upturned V, and "braced" means doubled up and interlocking. Gray's interest is part of a wider interest in genealogy. He seems to have carried the relationships of the noble families of England in his head. His copy of Clarendon's *History of the Civil War* in the Bodleian is full of marginalia, giving Christian names and further relationships to people mentioned in the text; unremarkable when done once or twice but astounding when it is repeated on page after page. There is a special gift involved in being able to relate a person to his grandparents' in-laws or even further across the family-tree, as anyone related to a member of a family history society will testify: it can be amazing or maddening. It does not, however, seem to have bothered Gray that the sculpting of the arms on the Bellingham and Parr tombs is very crudely done and badly spelt. Gray made another mistake in the dating of the Bellingham tomb, which is clearly dated 1533 on the brass. What may have happened, however, is that the tomb was restored in the nineteenth century and the brass with the date 1577 (which Gray gives) is now on the wall. The chapel itself, with the demise of the Bellingham family, is now used as a chapel for the local Border Regiment.

The castle is an energetic but rewarding walk to the east of the town. It seems to have decayed still further since Gray's day, since there are now only two towers still standing, one square and one round, and the curtain wall is much broken. It has received a fairly full de-medievalizing treatment in recent years, since it is now surrounded with a grit path as a kind of dry moat, and is fully equipped with floodlights, gas beacon, interpretative displays on low desks, and protected with soil erosion measures, fences, ladders and platforms. All well done, of course, but cumulatively it has an effect. The best of this modern furniture is a number of stone seats, masquerading as glacial erratic boulders, by Alain Ayer. The best of the fine view is not to the "fertile valley", which Gray saw and which is now filled with the spreading town, but away to the north to the first of the Lake District hills.

The trip to Sizergh should not have taken Gray long, since it is only a few miles south of Kendal, but it was a pity that he could not see inside, as we now can. The castle is basically a fourteenth-century pele tower, extended in Elizabethan times, with exceptionally fine interior carved woodwork on its chimney-pieces and balusters and panelling. It also has attractive gardens. It is still occupied by the Strickland family but is owned by the National Trust and open in the summer months. Gray appears to have walked from Sizergh down a lane in the direction of Sedgwick to the Kent at Force bridge. Here there is a waterfall across the river, not high or spectacular like High Force but still beautiful and impressive when the river is running full. Presumably it was recommended to Gray as a beautiful spot but he sounds disappointed, as if he had expected something more dramatic. West's explanation was "that the stream is much impaired in beauty since the forge was erected". If you go at the right time now (autumn), you can watch the salmon leap upstream here; a salmon leap has been constructed at the side of the fall and there is a viewing platform underneath the new motorway-link road bridge. On the river-banks *upstream* are the remains of the old gunpowder works started by John Wakefield in 1764. However, Gray definitely speaks of the forge as being *down* the river and so there must have been some small building, which has since disappeared, nearer the mouth of the river, to which the ore could have been brought by water. There was a plentiful supply of alder and birch for charcoal and the water-power was provided by the fast-flowing Kent. These were the conditions that made it worth importing iron-ore from Scotland. It is strange, however, that the forge should be seen as one of the sights. "The distant forge's swinging thump profound" is also part of the scene that Wordsworth records in the course of his *Evening Walk* some twenty years or so later, perhaps in imitation of Gray; he was writing of the bloomeries in the nearby woodlands of Furness. It is strange too that Gray should apocalyptically see the men as "dæmons", as Hardy's Tess and Angel saw the locomotive as an alien monster in the countryside a century later.

Levens is grander than Sizergh but also basically Elizabethan. It was bought by James Graham, a firm Jacobite supporter of James II, in 1688 and then descended, as a result of a lack of male heirs, first to Lord Suffolk, as Gray notes, and finally to the Bagot family, who live there now. It is best known for its topiary, originating from the work of King James II's gardener, M. Beaumont, who was found a job by the Catholic family after the 1688 revolution. Gray was very close to its mile-long avenue of oaks.

TAILPIECE: GRAY ON BIRDS

Impromptu couplet, composed during a walk:

There pipes the woodlark, and the song-thrush there
Scatters his loose notes in the waste of air.

Stanza from *The Pleasure arising from Vicissitude*:

But chief the skylark warbles high
His trembling thrilling ecstasy
And lessening from the dazzled sight
Melts into air and liquid light.

[From Gray, Collins and Goldsmith: The Complete Poems]

Overleaf: East View of Lancaster, by Joseph Farington.

DAY ELEVEN

Kendal to Lancaster

Oct: 10. went by *Burton* to Lancaster. W^d N:W: clouds & sun. 22m: very good country well enclosed & wooded with some common interspersed. pass'd at the foot of *Farlton-knot*, a high fell. 4 m: N: of Lancaster on a rising ground call'd *Bolton* (pron: *Bouton*)-*Wait* had a full view of *Cartmell-sands* with here and there a Passenger riding over them (it being low water) the points of Furness shooting far into the sea, & lofty mountains partly cover'd with clouds extending North of them. Lancaster also appear'd very conspicuous & fine, for its most distinguish'd features the Castle & Church, mounted on a green eminence, were all, that could be seen. woe is me! when I got thither, it was the second day of their fair. the Inn (in the principal street) was a great old gloomy house full of people, but I found tolerable quarters, & even slept two nights in peace.

Ascended the Castle-hill in a fine afternoon. it takes up the higher top of the eminence on wch it stands, & is irregularly round, encompassed with a deep mote. in front towards the Town is a magnificent Gothick Gateway, lofty & huge, the overhanging battlements are supported by a triple range of corbels, the intervals pierced thro' & shewing the day from above. on its top rise light watchtowers of small height. it opens below with a grand pointed arch: over this is a wrought tabernacle, doubtless once containing the Founder's figure, on one side a shield of France semy quarter'd with England, on the other the same with a label ermine for John of Gaunt D: of Lancaster. this opens to a court within, wch I did not much care to enter, being the County Gaol & full of Prisoners, both Criminals & Debtors. from this gateway the walls continue & join it to a vast square tower of great height, the lower part at least of remote antiquity, for it has small round-headed lights with plain short pillars on each side of them, there is a third tower also square & of less dimensions. this is all the castle. near it & but little lower stands the Church, a large & plain Gothic fabrick, the high square Tower at the West-end has been rebuilt of late years, but nearly in the same style. there are no ornaments of arms, &c: anywhere to be seen. within it is lightsome & spacious, but not one monument of antiquity, or piece of painted glass is left. from the Church-yard there is an extensive sea-view (for now the tide had almost cover'd the sands, & fill'd the river) & besides greatest part of Furness I could distinguish *Peel*-Castle on the isle of Fowdrey [Foulney], wch lies off its southern extremity. the Town is built on the slope & at the feet of Castle-hill more than twice the bigness of Aukland with many neat buildings of white stone, but a little disorderly in their positions ad libitum, like Kendal. many also extend below on the keys by the river-side, where a number of ships were moor'd, some of them three-mast vessels deck'd out with their colours in honor of the Fair. here is a good bridge of 4 arches over the *Lune*, wch runs (when the tide is out) in two streams divided by a bed of gravel, wch is not cover'd but in spring-tides. below the town it widens to near the breadth of ye Thames at London, & meets the sea at 5 or 6 m: distance to S:W:

COMMENTARY

ARTHUR Young in 1770 describes Lancaster as "a flourishing town, well situated for trade, of which it carries on a pretty brisk one, possessing about 100 sail of ships, some of them of a good burthen, for the *African* and *American* trades". It is not surprising therefore that Gray should find the "keys" full of activity, though he might have been surprised to find that some of the ships were slavers. These were small ships carrying 80-180 slaves from the West African coast to the West Indies. They were put out of business by larger ships and by an Act of Parliament of the 1770s which limited the trade to London, Bristol and Liverpool. There would not have been slaves for auction on the quayside but Dickens in years later sensed that the town was tainted by the trade.

> Mr Goodchild concedes Lancaster to be a pleasant place, a place dropped in the middle of a charming landscape, a place with a fine fragment of a castle, a place of lovely walks, a place possessing staid old houses richly fitted with old Honduras mahogany, which has grown so

dark with time that it seems to have got something a retrospective mirror quality into itself, and to show the visitor, in the depth of its grain, through all its polish, the hue of the wretched slaves who groaned long ago under old Lancaster merchants.

Some Georgian warehouses on St George's Quay survive from those days, as does the Custom House, "a fine Palladian job of 1764", as Pevsner calls it, and now the interesting and original Maritime Museum. However, it is the castle and the priory church which continue to dominate Lancaster from their still green eminence. One would have expected this church to have been elevated to full cathedral status by now (especially as the Catholics have their cathedral here now), since it is large and fine enough. The Victorians made up for the lack of medieval glass by glazing almost every window and there are plenty of fine eighteenth-century plaques, just too late for Gray, and a large number of military memorials testifying to the cost of empire, to make up for the lack of medieval tombs. The work on the tower, which Gray noticed, had been caused by over-ambitious churchwardens, who installed an exceptionally heavy peal of bells in 1743, causing the tower to start to collapse. It had to be taken down and was rebuilt completely in the old style in 1756. The finest things in the church are the carved choir stalls: Pevsner rates them "the most luxuriant canopies in the country". The carving is unbelievably ornate and collects the dust beautifully.

Next to the church, though turned the other way on, with its front gate facing the town, is the castle. It is best, as Gray did, to avoid an entry at this gate, as the castle, at least two-thirds of it, is still a working prison. Nevertheless, it is a magnificent affair, with its tabernacle, now containing a statue of John of Gaunt and, high above the dark, forbidding walls, its machicolations. One does not often have the chance to use this fine word, which refers to the openings under a projecting parapet through which missiles could be dropped. On the west side of the castle is the Shire Hall, containing the Courts of Justice. These were built some thirty years after Gray's visit, in order to renovate the decaying structure and to provide purpose-built courts and cells. The two court-rooms, still in use, are in an attractive pre-Victorian Gothic. The prison is due to close in a few years and the castle then will able to revert to its true role as a tourist attraction.

There is indeed an extensive seaward view from the churchyard but it was a hazy day when I was there and I certainly could not see Peel Castle, fifteen miles away across Morecambe Bay. It does stand up well on its point of land but Gray must have had exceptional sight, a very clear day, or a spy-glass. He does not mention Coniston Old Man and the Langdale Pikes and Helvellyn, which are visible in most weathers, a view which seems to bring the Lake District close.

Gray did not have the advantage of being able to climb the Ashton Memorial, a huge monument about a mile east of the town centre, which everyone who passes Lancaster must now see. It was built between 1906 and 1909 to the memory of the wife of Lord Ashton (who made a fortune from oilcloth), and is second only in size to the Albert Memorial in comparable buildings. Pevsner calls it "the grandest monument in England" and it is both imposing and beautiful. It also gives a superlative view. From the viewing gallery here I *could* see Peel Castle, though I used a monocular to do so and it is somewhat dwarfed now by the cranes and buildings of Vickers Armstrong shipyard in next-door Barrow and by the nuclear power station at nearby Heysham.

Gray seems to have enjoyed himself here, wandering about the then compact but hilly heart of this still largely eighteenth-century town, despite the fair which he managed to hit upon; this latter was a three-day affair held three times a year in April, July, and October, primarily for the sale of cattle.

> ## TAILPIECE: ADVICE TO A FRIEND TRAVELLING IN SCOTLAND
>
> See your sheets air'd yourself. Eat mutton or hard-eggs. Touch no fried things. If they are broil'd, boil'd, or roasted, say that from a child you have eat no butter, & beg they would not rub any over your meat. There is honey, or orange-marmalade, or currant-jelly, wch may be eaten with toasted bread, or the thin oat-cakes, for breakfast. Dream not of milk. Ask your landlord to set down, & help off with your wine. Never scold at anybody, especially at Gentlemen, or Ladies.
>
> *[From Notes included as an Appendix to Gray's Correspondence p.1246]*

Overleaf: Lancaster Sand, by J.M.W.Turner.

DAY TWELVE

Poulton & the Sands

Oct: 11. W^d S:W: clouds & sun. warm & a fine dappled sky. cross'd the river & walk'd over a peninsula 3 miles to the village of *Pooton* wch stands on the beach. an old Fisherman mending his nets (while I enquired about the danger of passing those sands) told me in his dialect a moving story, how a brother of the trade, a *Cockler* (as he styled him, driving a little cart with two daughters (women grown) in it, & his Wife on horseback following, set out one day to pass the 7 mile sands, as they had frequently been used to do, for nobody in the village knew them better than the old Man did. when they were about half way over, a thick fog rose, & as they advanced, they found the water much deeper than they expected. the old man was puzzled, he stop'd, & said he would go a little way to find some mark he was acquainted with. they staid a little while for him, but in vain. they call'd aloud, but no reply. at last the young women press'd their mother to think, where they were, & go on. she would not leave the place, she wander'd about forlorn & amazed, she would not quit her horse, & get into the cart with them. they determined after much time wasted to turn back, & give themselves up to the guidance of the horses. the old Woman was soon wash'd off and perish'd. the poor Girls clung close to their cart, & the horse sometimes wading & sometimes swimming brought them back to land alive, but senseless with terror & distress & unable for many days to give any account of themselves. the bodies of their parents were found soon after (next ebb); that of the Father a very few paces distant from the spot, where he had left them.[3]

 In the afternoon wander'd about the town & by the key till it grew dark. a little rain fell.

---

3. In the Murray MS there followed: " & all the village mourned over them", which was crossed out.

COMMENTARY

IT WAS possible in 1769 for Gray to wander down through more or less open countryside to the village of Poulton, for Morecambe and Heysham did not exist at that time: they came later with the development of an Irish ferry terminal and the coming of the railway in the 1840s. He must have ruled out a Sands crossing because of his inability to ride or perhaps because he was on his own. Nevertheless, he seems to have been fascinated by the crossing, as he had spent some time on the previous day watching people coming across, and now he came down to gaze at the bay. The major reason for journeying by Lancaster for most travellers was to be able to cut across the Sands and perhaps that was why it was originally on Gray's itinerary too. The Sands provided the shortest, easiest, and most picturesque route into the Furness peninsula and the Lake District from the south, though there was no regular coach crossing until a special light-weight diligence, carrying three passengers, was introduced in 1781. Thomas West in his *Guide* (1778) declared that "with proper guides, crossing of the sands in summer is thought a journey of little more danger than any other". Ann Radcliffe, Thomas de Quincey, and Harriet Martineau all came this way, but Thomas Pennant found it "a melancholy ride" in 1770: "The prospect on all sides quite savage, high barren hills indented by sea, and dreary wet sands, rendered more horrible by the approach of night". Pennant might well feel apprehensive, for the Sands crossing had an ominous reputation, supported by repeated records of "drowned on the Sands" in the early parish registers of Cartmel Priory. One tablet on the church floor at the Priory records the death by drowning of Robert Harrison on Lancaster Sands on 13th January, 1780, at the age of 24 - and of the similar death of his mother in the same spot, exactly one year later: there must be a story to this coincidence.

The problem was, and is, partly one of time. The crossing was considered safe only when the tide had been ebbing for four hours, or up to two hours before high tide, leaving six hours for the crossing, twice a day. Time could be lost by such hazards as sudden fog or quicksands, and so there was always a strong element of risk involved. Three rivers had to be forded in a full crossing, the Keer, the Kent, and the Leven, and their courses constantly shifted, leaving "lyrings", half-filled channels, which were very dangerous.

Some of the apprehension that Gray may have felt comes out in Cockin's description of the crossing included as a note in second and later editions of West's *Guide*.

What most attracts the traveller is not the objects of the surrounding country (though they are fine) but *the sands themselves*. For when he has got a few miles from the shore the nature of the plain on which he treads, cannot but suggest a series of ideas of a more sublime kind than those of rural elegance, and which will therefore gain a superior attention. The plain is then seemingly immense in extent, continued on a dead level, and uniform in appearance. As he pursues his *often-trackless* way, he will recollect, that probably but a few hours before, the whole expanse was covered with some fathoms of water, and that in a few more it will as certainly be covered again. At the same time he may also perceive, on his left hand, the retreated ocean ready to obey the mysterious laws of its irresistible movement, without any visible barrier to stay it a moment where it is. These last considerations, though they may not be sufficient to alarm, must yet be able to rouse the mind to a state of more than ordinary attention; which cooperating with the other singular ideas of the prospect, must affect it in a very sublime and unusual manner. This the bare appearance of the sands will do. But when the traveller reaches the side of the Eau [Lancashire dialect for river or canal], these affections will be greatly increased. He there drops down a gentle descent to the edge of a broad and seemingly impassable river, where the only remains he can perceive of the surrounding lands are the tops of distant mountains, and where a solitary being on horseback (like some ancient genius of the deep) is described hovering on its brink, or encountering the stream with gentle steps, in order to conduct him through it. When fairly entered into the water, if a stranger to the scene, and he do not feel himself touched with some of the most pleasing emotions, I should think him destitute of common sensibility. For in the midst of apparently great danger, he will soon find that there is really none at all; and the complacency which must naturally result from this consideration, will be heightened to an unusual degree, by observing, during his passage, the anxious and faithful instinct of his beast; and the friendly behaviour and aspect of his guide. All the fervours of grateful thankfulness will then be raised, and if with the usual perquisite to his venerable conductor, he can forget to convey his blessing, who would not conclude him to want one essential requisite for properly enjoying the tour of the lakes?

A walk across the Sands now is less likely to bring you so close to the sublime. On a sunny day there will be hundreds of other walkers, old and young (with their dogs), chattering and laughing, apparently unaware of any danger, trusting completely to the guide, who has marked out the route the day before and who has a friend with a tractor and trailer in reserve for emergencies. Splashing through the rivers becomes a lark, after the first few steps accustom you to the wet and reassure you about the depth and firmness. Yet, at the very least, it is a most unusual and enjoyable walk, with that long, flat, slightly menacing horizon to the south and the sombre outline of the Lake District hills to the north. When you are out in the middle, the vast expanse is oppressive: to be caught out there would be to be without hope. The route across, with its zig-zags round soft sands and inlets and river-crossing is so obviously a mystery that no-one surely would attempt to cross without a guide. There is a sensation out there, as you walk on a strange element, not firm land and with deep water not far away, which makes one share Gray's apprehension.

It would be interesting to know what was going through Gray's mind as he walked down to the village of Poulton. Was it just interest that brought him down to look across this impressive estuarine bay, or was it a nagging desire to see the route across the Sands that he had not dared to take? In recording the story of the old man and his wife, Gray may have been trying to convince himself that he did the right thing, as well as revealing his own taste for a tragic anecdote.

TAILPIECE: A GRAY ANECDOTE

In the year 1688 my Lord Peterborough had a great mind to be well with Lady Sandwich (Mrs Bonfoy's old friend). There was a woman, who kept a great Coffee-house in Pall Mall, & she had a miraculous Canary-Bird, that piped twenty tunes. Lady S: was fond of such things, had heard of, & seen the bird. Lord P: came to the woman, and offered her a large sum of money for it; but she was rich, & proud of it, and would not part with it for love or money. However, he watched the bird narrowly, observed all its marks and features, went and bought just such another, sauntered into the coffee-room, took his opportunity when no-one was by, slipped the wrong bird into the cage, & went off undiscovered to make my Lʸ. Sandwich happy. This was just about the time of the Revolution; and a good while after, going into the same Coffee-house again, he saw his bird there, and said, well, I reckon, you would give your ears now, that you had taken my money. Money! (Says the woman) no, nor ten times that money now; dear little creature; for if your Lᴾ. will believe me (as I am a Christian it is true,) it has moped & moped, and never once opened its pretty lips, since the day that the *poor king* went away!

(From a letter to James Brown, 9 Feb. 1761.)

Overleaf: Hornby Castle, after Samuel Buck.

DAY THIRTEEN

Lancaster to Settle

Oct: 11.[4] W^d N:E: sky gloomy, then gleams of sunshine. set out for *Settle* by a fine turnpike road, 29 miles. Rich & beautiful enclosed country diversified with frequent villages & churches, very unequal ground, & on the left the river Lune winding in a deep valley, its hanging banks clothed with fine woods, thro' wch you catch long reaches of the water, as the road winds about at a considerable height above it. pass'd the *Park* (Hon: Mr Clifford's, a catholick) in the most picturesque part of the way. the grounds between him & the river are indeed charming: the house is ordinary, & the park nothing but a rocky fell scatter'd over with ancient hawthorns. came to *Hornby* a little Town on the river Wenning, over wch a handsome bridge is now in building. the Castle in a lordly situation attracted me, so I walk'd up the hill to it. first presents itself a large but ordinary white Gentleman's house sash'd. behind it rises the ancient Keep built by Edward Stanley, Lord Mounteagle (inscribed *Helas et quand?*) he died about 1524 in Henry 8th's time. it is now a shell only, tho' rafters are laid within it as for flooring. I went up a winding stone-staircase in one corner to the leads, & at the angle is a single hexagon watch-tower rising some feet higher, fitted up in the tast of a modern *Toot* with sash-windows in gilt frames, & a stucco cupola, & on the top a vast gilt eagle by Mr *Charteris*, the present Possessor. but he has not lived here since the year 1745, when the people of Lancaster insulted him, threw stones into his coach, & almost made his wife (Lady Katherine Gordon) miscarry. since that he has built a great ugly house of red stone (thank God it is not in England) near Haddington, wch I remember to have passed by. he is the 2^d Son of the Earl of Wemyss, & brother to the Ld Elcho, Grandson to Col: Charteris, whose name he bears.

---

4. Gray made a mistake in the dating of this day (in fact, the 12th), which affected subsequent days until the 14th.

From the leads of the Tower there is a fine view of the country round, & much wood near the castle. Ingleborough, wch I had seen before distinctly at Lancaster to N:E: was now compleatly wrap'd in clouds all but its summit, wch might have been easily mistaken for a long black cloud too, fraught with an approaching storm. now our road begun gradually to mount toward the *Apennine*, the trees growing less, & thinner of leaves, till we came to Ingleton 18 m: it is a pretty village situated very high & yet in a valley at the foot of that huge creature of God *Ingleborough*. two torrents cross it with great stones roll'd along their bed instead of water: over them are two handsome arches flung. here at a little ale-house were Sr Bellingcam Graham & Mr Parker, L^d of ye Manour (one of them 6 feet ½ high, & the other as much in breadth) come to dine.

The nipping air (tho' the afternoon was growing very bright) now taught us, we were in Craven. the road was all up & down (tho' no where very steep). to the left were mountain-tops (Weryside), to the right a wide valley (all inclosed ground) & beyond it high hills again. in approaching Settle the crags on the left drew nearer to our way, till we ascended *Brunton-brow*, into a chearful valley (tho' thin of trees) to *Giggleswick* a village with a small piece of water by its side cover'd over with coots. near it a Church, wch belongs also to *Settle* & half a mile farther having passed the *Ribble* over a bridge arrived at *Settle*. it is a small market-town standing directly under a rocky fell. there are not a dozen good-looking houses, the rest are old & low with little wooden portico's in front. my inn pleased me much (tho' small) for the neatness & civility of the good Woman that kept it, so I lay there two nights, & went [to visit *Gordale-Scar*].

COMMENTARY

GRAY took the turnpike road for Richmond out of Lancaster, following at first the south bank of the Lune. The Honourable Mr Edward Clifford's Park (or East Park Hall, as it is named on early maps) must have been close to the road and river; it has now disappeared, leaving only a pair of gate-lodges at the entrance to Old Hall Farm. Gray repeatedly picks out Catholic families for special mention and there may be a touch of animosity or suspicion in this. There is certainly some scorn for the subdued fashion in which the Catholic gentry were obliged to live:"the house is ordinary and the Park nothing". There is a traditional belief that Gray stopped in these first few miles to admire the view over the river and there is a project to site a Gray's Seat to mark the spot. If he did stop, he does not make it very clear where, but it might well have been near the Crook o'Lune, above the present road on what is now private land. The deep valley with the curving river within its hanging banks is still a beautiful place but the vegetation has grown too much to offer a view. West, who was looking east to Ingleborough from a slightly different point, called it "one of the finest afternoon rural views in England", a superlative curiously qualified by the word "afternoon". West, however, also complained in finicky fashion about Gray's choice of station, claiming that Gray was "a quarter mile too low and somewhat too much to the left". Turner also found his own viewpoint along this stretch for a painting looking south-east over the river to the city in the distance; he seems to have found a field on the road to Halton for this and then to have gone to the main road for another view up to Hornby. One might now complain that the "station" has lost the openness which gave it its early fame and that it has been tamed out of sublimity with paths and picnic places.

Gray may have been attracted to Hornby by his knowledge of the part played by the original Edward Stanley in turning the tide at Flodden. He makes it sound as if he walked up to the Castle and set about climbing the apparently semi-derelict pele-tower without permit or guide. More probably his servant Stephen located the curators and he was shown the way. Even so, it must have taken some nerve to climb up to the leads. The "toot" was an apparently elaborate gazebo or lookout, then fashionable, the word coming from a slang word, "tout", to watch. The place is very private now, and very different. In front of the old tower there is now a Victorian mock-castle, built by a (presumably) successful financier. The mysterious Stanley motto is no longer visible on the walls, though there is a Stanley emblem remaining: a claw, but no eagle. The building has been through the hands of many families in its long history. Fortunately the Charteris who owned it in Gray's day was not the notorious Charteris who was guilty of rape, among various infamies, and who died universally detested. It is a stunning site, overlooking a curve in the Lune, and looking from the bridge, as Pevsner says, "as if seen in a picture book".

Ingleton, which Gray reached after some un-noted travel up the valley of the Wenning, still has some prettiness, though it has grown too much to have survived unscathed. It is just not possible now to sum up places in the simple terms that Gray used. The railway has been and departed, leaving a colossal viaduct straddling the valley; modern roads have bypassed the village with its steep inclines, leaving uglier bridges. Its heyday must have been the 1920s when the Misses Dodgson could advertise their residential boarding house with bath and electric light and the Ingleboro Hotel could cater for select parties of up to 200 and the Cinema would put on special shows for wet days. But it is still a staging post and a magnet for day-visitors, wanting to see the caverns and waterfalls or to walk up Ingleborough; the eroded footpath to its summit is visible from a considerable distance.

Why should Gray call Ingleborough, "that huge creature of God"? It does have the shape of a brooding monster but there is more in the phrase. There is a curious mixture of attraction and repulsion, a feeling similar to Blake's feeling for the tiger. "What immortal hand or eye / Could frame thy fearful symmetry." Gray's first travels among mountains, in 1739 to the Grande Chartreuse, had produced similar feelings of fear leading to religious awe. "There are certain scenes that would awe an atheist into belief, without the help of other argument" (Letter to West, 16 Nov, 1739). He spoke in the same terms after his visit to the Highlands of Scotland in 1765.

> I am returned from Scotland charmed with my expedition; it
> is of the Highlands I speak; the Lowlands are worth seeing once, but the
> mountains are ecstatic, and ought to be visited in pilgrimage once a
> year. None but these monstrous creatures of God know how to join so

much beauty with so much horror. A fig for your poets, painters, gardeners, and clergymen, that have not been among them; their imagination can be made up of nothing but bowling-greens, flowering shrubs, horse-ponds, Fleet ditches, shell grottoes, and Chinese rails. Then I had so beautiful an autumn, Italy could hardly produce a nobler scene, and this so sweetly contrasted with that perfection of nastiness, and total want of accommodation, that only Scotland can supply. Oh you would have blessed your self. I shall certainly go again; what a pity it is I cannot draw, nor describe, nor ride on horseback (Letter to Mason, undated).

Gray's "Weryside" is clearly a mishearing of Whernside, one of the three peaks for which this area is now famous, the other one (besides Ingleborough) being Pen-y-ghent, which Gray later records as having seen as well. In fact, Whernside, at 2414 feet, is the highest of the three. All these hills are to the north of his route but he also records Pendle Hill to the south, though he appears unaware or uninterested in its connection with the trials of the seventeenth-century witches.

Giggleswick no longer has its lake or its coots, the former having been drained to provide a golf course, though some of the greens were reverting to their underwater days when I passed by. Settle, however, miraculously still has at least one wooden portico, as I discovered by knocking on one, to the alarm of the residents inside. The town must have tried to smarten itself, for there are now a considerable number of beautifully elaborate stone porticoes. At least Gray was made happy and contented there by the neatness and civility of the good woman at the inn: good for him as well as good for her!

Overleaf: Gordale Scar, by James Ward

DAY FOURTEEN

Gordale Scar

Oct: 12. [From Settle I went] to visit *Gordale-Scar*. W^d N:E: day gloomy & cold. it lay but 6 m: from Settle, but that way was directly over a Fell, & it might rain, so I went round in a chaise the only way one could get near it in a carriage, wch made it full 13 m: & half of it such a road! but I got safe over it, so there's an end, & came to *Malham* (pronounce *Maum*) a village in the bosom of the mountains seated in a wild & dreary valley. from thence I was to walk a mile over very rough ground, a torrent rattling along on the left hand. on the cliffs above hung a few goats: one of them danced & scratched an ear with its hind-foot in a place where I would not have stood stock-still

- for all beneath the moon.

as I advanced the crags seem'd to close in, but discover'd a narrow entrance turning to the left between them. I followed my guide a few paces, & lo, the hills open'd again into no large space, & then all farther way is bar'd by a stream, that at the height of about 50 feet gushes from a hole in the rock, & spreading in large sheets over its broken front dashes from steep to steep, & then rattles away in a torrent down the valley. the rock on the left rises perpendicular with stubbed yew-trees & shrubs, staring from its side to the height of at least 300 feet. but these are not the thing! it is that to the right, under wch you stand to see the fall, that forms the principal horror of the place. from its very base it begins to slope forwards over you in one black & solid mass without any crevice in its surface, & overshadows half the area below with its dreadful canopy. when I stood at (I believe) full 4 yards distance from its foot, the drops wch perpetually distill from its brow, fell on my head, & in one part of its top more exposed to the weather there are loose stones that hang in air, & threaten visibly some idle Spectator with instant destruction. it is safer to shelter yourself close to its bottom, & trust the mercy of that enormous mass, wch nothing but an earthquake can stir. the gloomy uncomfortable day well suited the savage aspect of the place, & made it still more formidable. I stay'd there (not without shuddering) a quarter of an hour, & thought my trouble richly paid, for the impression will last for life. at the alehouse where I dined in Malham, Vivares, the landscape-painter, had lodged for a week or more. Smith & Bellers had also been there, & two prints of Gordale have been engraved by them. return'd to my comfortable inn. night fine, but windy & frosty.

COMMENTARY

GRAY, with his mind totally absorbed by the scale of the natural wonder he had been brought to see, does not seem to have had eyes for the rich vegetation of this area. Nor does he seem to have been aware that one of his undoubted heroes, John Ray, the seventeenth-century naturalist, had been this way before him. Ray visited Gordale and Malham in 1671 and discovered for himself specimens of Jacob's Ladder, as well as dark-red helleborine. Ray had also visited Ullswater but, for his part, he kept his eyes on the plants and did not look at the scenery.

Gray's description of Gordale has been ambivalently assessed by Margaret Drabble as "perhaps one of the most complete illustrations of the literary concept of the sublime". She does not seem to mean this as praise, for she goes on to write critically about Gray's outlook.

> This is one of the few passages that has actually made me go and look at a place, and the experience was interesting: the Scar is less frightening than Gray makes it appear, but it is also more beautiful. Of course, Gray saw it on a gloomy uncomfortable day and I have seen it only in good weather; nevertheless, it appeared at once less vast and savage and more deserving of attention. It also struck me that any post-Freudian would of necessity see this landscape in terms of sexual imagery - the hollow cavern, the gushing water, the secrecy of the approach - and would remark how notably this vocabulary is missing from Gray and Gilpin, though it is present enough in Milton, whose references to "the womb of water", to genial moisture, to heaving mountains, laps and entrails and bosoms, to shaggy hills and bushes

with frizzled hair and hills with "hairie sides", make the creation of the world sound a thoroughly sexual process: he sees the world as a living being, conceived, gestated, born, passing through unadorned childhood to the springing tender grass of puberty. This organic vision was lost for a century and a half after Milton: it was deeply inaccessible to Gray....

Even if this is true, and it is urged with feeling, it does not mean that Gray and his contemporaries did not have something else, awe, that we also need. This passage clearly needs the adoption of a historical perspective and a sympathetic interpretation of the diction (especially of the word "horror"), as was the case with the day in Borrowdale.

As with Margaret Drabble, this is one of the few passages that has actually made me go and look at a place that I had not been to before. I set out early (7.45) on a Sunday morning, determined to have the place to myself. Solitude is, to my mind, essential to the effect and it is not easily obtained, since the Scar is now a tourist honeypot. Gray's description is excellent. You do come upon the Scar suddenly, turning a corner and finding a huge wall of rock in front of you, and, as Gray says, it is then the right wall, rather than the left one, which is the more fearsome. The right hand wall overhangs and drips water ten feet or so from the bottom. Between the two walls a noisy waterfall pours down from half way up. It feels like being at the bottom of Gaping Gill, with the roof fallen in, though some geologists now say it is not, in fact, a collapsed pot-hole. I did find it an awesome place, more savage than beautiful, and I did feel a kind of fear. There are, after all, several kinds of fear. There is the fear of stone-fall from the heights above, which anyone in their right senses feels. There is the fear that I felt as I started to climb the waterfall, by the wrong route, on steep, wet, slippery rock, the fear which is a lack of nerve. But there is another kind of fear where you just feel daunted or overwhelmed. I have felt that fear when climbing in the Himalayas; I have felt it on a few occasions of freak weather conditions in the Lake District; and I felt it here. The surprise of the discovery is part of the reason; the roar of the water is another; the cold and the claustrophobia of the situation at the bottom of the cliff is

124   *Thomas Gray's Journal*

another; and being alone in it and undisturbed for more than a quarter of an hour is another. It would not have had that effect half an hour later, for there were the tell-tale signs of modern visitors in numbers: discarded cans and litter, pegs and karabiners left by climbers half way up the cliff, signposts and warnings ("Difficult climb up: take care"), eroded paths. The yew-trees have survived. The goats were enjoying richer pastures lower down on the day I came. Swifts were attacking the rock-faces in soaring Tornado-like runs.

I eventually found the right route up the waterfall, a perfectly safe scramble to the left of the main fall, though Gray could never have attempted it. It is worth going on, because it develops into a classic walk. From the top of the fall there is a good view down into the gorge. Then the path comes out onto soft springy turf, leading, more or less on the level, to Malham Tarn, a beautiful lake, worth a visit in its own right. It is not difficult to locate a path south from here down to Malham Cove, a huge limestone amphitheatre, in some ways more impressive than the Scar itself, though much more open. By the time I got there, the cars, minibuses, and coaches had arrived. I have never, ever, seen so many people in open countryside - a continuous stream of people walking up from the village to the Cove: a group of foreign school-children chattering noisily, a band of professional ramblers in the latest outdoor equipment, a family discussing the characterization in "Lord of the Rings", a group of scruffy climbers with clusters of slings, nuts, ropes, various stout mothers trying to stop toddlers disappearing down the grikes, the cracks in the limestone pavement. I doubt whether any natural phenomenon can withstand that kind of attack and still make any kind of aesthetic impact. No-one, I may add, in either inn in the village, not even at the Lister Arms, where Gray probably dined, had heard of Thomas Gray or of the visiting painters.

They should have known of Thomas Girtin, James Ward, and Turner as well, all of whom helped to make Gordale famous. Ward, in particular, painted a massive canvas (131 in. by 166 in.) to try to convey the terrifying appearance of the crag. Incredibly, the painting, which normally hangs in the Tate, dominating its room, has been removed from the walls (presumably because it occupies too much space!) and will not be replaced for some years yet. Ward did do some preparatory sketches and a small one, very dark and obscure and not doing it justice, can be seen in the City Art Gallery in Leeds. Geoffrey Grigson calls the big painting "a highly effective image of the sublime". Edward Dayes, a few years before Ward, declared that "the lover of drawing will be delighted with this place: immensity and horror are its inseparable companions, uniting to form subjects of the most awful cast". Ward's painting is one of the great images of Romanticism but it has had a chequered history. The British Museum, to whom it was bequeathed, soon found it too big for its walls and took it down and gave it back. After a public outcry, it was re-bought for the nation but it is not surprising, after that history, that it should be back in the cellar.

TAILPIECE: FEAR AND BEAUTY IN SCOTLAND

We ferried over the Tummel in order to get into Marshal Wade's road (wch leads from Dunkeld to Inverness) & continued our way along it toward the north. the road is excellent, but dangerous enough in conscience. the river often running directly under us at the bottom of a precipice 200 feet deep, sometimes masqued indeed by wood, that finds means to grow where I could not stand: but very often quite naked & without any defence. in such places we walked for miles together partly for fear, & partly to admire the beauty of the country, wch the beauty of the weather set off to the greatest advantage.

[From a letter to Dr Wharton, 30 Sept. 1765]

Overleaf: Kirkstall Abbey, by Thomas Smith of Derby

DAY FIFTEEN

Settle to Otley

Oct: 13. Went to Skipton, 16 miles. W^d N:E: gloomy, at one o'clock a little sleet falls. from several parts of the road, & in many places about Settle I saw at once the three famous hills of this country, Ingleborough, Penigent, & Pendle, the first is esteem'd the highest. their features are hard to describe, but I could trace their outline with a pencil.

Craven after all is an unpleasing country, when seen from a height. its valleys are chiefly wide & either marshy, or enclosed pasture with a few trees. numbers of black cattle are fatted here, both of the Scotch breed, & a larger sort of oxen with great horns. there is little cultivated grounds, except a few oats.

[Oct: 14. W^d N.E. gloomy. at noon a few grains of sleet fell, then bright & clear.] Went thro' Long Preston & Gargrave to *Skipton* 16 miles. it is a pretty large Market-Town in a valley with one very broad street gently sloping downwards from the Castle, wch stands at the head of it. this is one of our good Countesse's buildings, but on old foundations: it is not very large, but of a handsome antique appearance with round towers, a grand gateway, bridge & mote, & many old trees about it, in good repair, & kept up, as a habitation of the Earl of Thanet, tho' he rarely comes thither. what with the sleet & a foolish dispute about chaises, that delay'd me, I did not see the inside of it, but went on 15 miles to *Ottley*. first up *Shode-bank*, the steepest hill I ever saw a road carried over in England, for it mounts in a strait line (without any other repose for the horses, than by placing stones every now & then behind the wheels) for a full mile. then the road goes on a level along the brow of this high hill over Rumbald-moor, till it gently descends into Wharfdale: so they call the Vale of the Wharf, & a beautiful vale it is, well-wooded, well-cultivated, well-inhabited, but with high crags at a distance, that border the green country on either hand. thro' the midst of it deep, clear, full to the brink, & of no inconsiderable breadth runs in long windings the river. How it comes to pass that it should be so fine & copious a stream here, & at Tadcaster (so much lower) should have nothing but a wide stony channel without water, I can not tell you. I pass'd through *Long-Addingham, Ilkley* (pronounce *Eecla*) distinguished by a lofty brow of loose rocks to the right, *Burley*, a neat & pretty village among trees. on the opposite side of the river lay *Middleton*-Lodge, belonging to a Catholick Gentleman of that name; *Weston*, a venerable stone fabrick with large offices, of Mr Vavasor, the meadows in front gently descending to the water, & behind a great & shady wood; Farnley (Mr Fawke's) a place like the last, but larger, & rising higher on the side of the hill. *Ottley* is a large airy Town, with clean but low rustick buildings, & a bridge over the Wharf. I went into its spatious Gothic Church, wch has been new-roof'd with a flat stucco ceiling. in a corner of it is the monument of Tho: Ld Fairfax, & Helen Aske, his Lady, descended from the Cliffords & Lattimers, as her epitaph says. the figures not ill-cut particularly his in armour, but bare-headed, lie on the tomb. I take them for the Grand Parents of the famous Sr Tho: Fairfax.

COMMENTARY

IT IS not so easy or pleasant to follow Gray on his last day, because he was on the move and modern roads do not permit one to travel in the same leisurely style, stopping and looking at will: this is particularly true of the A65. Gray is also behaving in a different way. He is tending to list places, castles, houses, churches, reverting to a kind of cultural collecting not so different from train-spotting. With a volume of Pevsner's county architectural guides in the car, one can still imitate this, noting the monuments, placing the period, making the historical connections; the difference with Gray was that it was all in his head. It is a pleasant pursuit, with aesthetic as well as intellectual rewards, but not in the end as uplifting as those insights about mountain scenery.

Gray's description of Skipton - "one very broad street gently sloping downward from the castle" - remains recognizable in Pevsner's contemporary description: " What remains in one's memory about

Skipton is the High Street, opening funnelwise to the church, and the castle entrance with its fat round towers". The houses in the high street are almost all nineteenth century and later but the mighty gatehouse of the castle still dominates. Gray may again have been shy of entering an aristocratic house but there is no problem now, as the castle is open to the public and one can see what Gray missed: an "exceedingly pretty" (according to Pevsner) seventeenth-century grotto-room lined with shells (now less pretty because used as a ticket office) and the "extremely picturesque" Conduit Court (dating back to Norman times), dwarfed by its magnificent yew tree. The good repair of the castle is due mainly to the industry of Lady Anne Clifford in the mid-seventeenth century - "our good Countess", as Gray familiarly refers to her - and to the present private owners who have renovated and adapted it (in most instances) discreetly. It is a fine castle to visit because it is (unusually) fully roofed and beautifully sited by the river. What Gray was able to do as he looked at castles and churches was relate them to a context of political and genealogical history and so make sense of them. This kind of informed observation is, of course, the secret of all such visiting and viewing.

If Gray had no time to visit the castle, he clearly had no time to look at the parish church either. He would have enjoyed the Clifford tombs and the magnificent Jacobean carved font-cover. He might now be surprised to find the Honeypot tea-room and refectory as an annexe.

Gray's worrying hill is now more difficult to locate. The old road climbed steeply up on to the moor from 400 feet to 1100 feet in the space of about a mile, in an almost straight line. It is certainly very steep, though it probably does not justify Gray's claim that it was the steepest hill in England; he was quick to use a superlative where he saw it as some kind of praise. It was re-routed at the beginning of the nineteenth century and the old road fell into disuse. The beginning of the road survives as Short Bank Road, on a housing estate on the edge of Skipton, but then dies out into a bridle path. Only a toll cottage is left at the bottom as a relic of the old obstacle, and some of the old stone setts. The line of the road can be picked up again, spectacularly, where it crosses the Draughton-Silsden road on Rombalds Moor. It runs straight as a die, probably following an old Roman road, across the very top of the moor, with superb views down to the valley on the north side. There is still a very old milestone marking the cross-roads: " To Skipton 3 Miles To Addingham 3 Miles". It is odd that Gray did not complain about the hill in Ingleton, which seems just as steep, though much shorter; that hill is still called Bell Horse Hill because coaches had to ring for help with the horses.

Some of Gray's prejudices and individual tastes appear in passing references: in his noting of a "Catholick gentleman", as if he were some sort of tolerated alien, and in his interest in the Fairfax family, revealing his fascination with the events of the Civil War (his copy of Clarendon's *History of the Civil War* is heavily annotated). Something of Gray's personality appears too in the curious remark about the "foolish dispute about chaises that delay'd me". One may guess that it was "foolish" because he had lost the argument and knew that he shouldn't have done: some rascal had out-faced him and obliged him to pay more than he should have done. One can also see Gray apprehensive about everyone's safety, as the stones were placed behind the wheels on Shode Bank.

Middleton Lodge is now swallowed up in the suburbs of Ilkley but Weston and Farnley Halls are still visible, high on the north bank of the Wharfe. Weston is, as Gray says, a very old house with extensive outbuildings, and a medieval church, which he probably couldn't see in the trees. It was one of the residences of the Catholic Vavasour family, a family going back to the Conquest, one of whom was knighted at Flodden. The house is a little island of peace down a cul-de-sac. Farnley is also safe down a forbidding drive and behind an encircling wall. Its very grand south front, in fact, dates from 1786, after Gray, but the house always had a dominant position, looking down over meadows to the Wharfe. It was the home of the Fawkes family, a later member of which made Turner welcome and had some influence on him. Another fine eighteenth-century house now looks down from the north bank, Denton Hall, looking very like Dalemain, but that too came just after Gray (in 1770).

The typically eighteenth-century fascination with water revives this passage, with the river "deep, clear, full to the brim" in its "well-wooded, well-cultivated, well-inhabited vale". The river still is deep and full but the valley is now too well-inhabited, its roads too busy, and its towns too cluttered. The church at Otley, which Gray found so interesting, is fortunately positioned beside a car-park, and, as at Skipton, there is an integral (and excellent) tea-room. Inside the church itself, besides the Fairfax tomb with its armoured knight and virtuous lady, are many tombs of the Fawkes family from Farnley. The feel of the church, however, is of a different age: almost all the glass is Victorian and the eighteenth-century box pews have gone, as has the stucco-ceiling which Gray mentions. Gray does not make it clear what he thought of this ceiling but it sounds rather as if he accepted it as an "improvement". What now seem curious attitudes prevailed towards medieval architecture at the time and it was not uncommon to hide fine medieval roofs behind warmer plaster ceilings: Carlisle Cathedral's hammer-beam roof was hidden behind a false roof by Dean Lyttleton in the 1760s, only to emerge a hundred years later.

Of course, this was not actually the end of Gray's journey. Gray in fact continued past Kirkstall Abbey, which greatly impressed him and which he described in a later letter. "The gloom of these ancient cells, the shade & verdure of the landscape, the glittering & murmur of the stream, the lofty towers & long perspectives of the church in the midst of a clear bright day, detain'd me for many hours & were the truest subjects for my glass I have met with anywhere." He stayed the night in that "smoky ugly busy town of Leeds" and went on to his friend Mason's at York, Mason providentially being away at the time. After two days there he returned to Cambridge, reaching "home" on 22nd October, "having met with no rain to signify". The sunny weather without must have helped to produce sunny weather within, for Gray's mood is benign throughout.

Overleaf: View of Derwentwater, by Thomas Smith

CONCLUSION

The Discovery of the Lake District

SO GRAY returned home with these notes in two (perhaps three) notebooks, which he later copied into four letters to Dr Thomas Wharton, so that his friend should know what he had missed. He seems never to have had in mind any further audience, no intention of turning his "journal" into a book, no awareness of having written anything out of the ordinary. Why should we take it any more seriously?

One reason is that people at the time very quickly took it seriously. Mason published the "journal" in its letter form as an appendix to the collected *Works* in 1775 and from there it was borrowed as an appendix to West's *Guide to the Lakes* in 1780. It rapidly had a wide and influential currency. The other reason is that it is still frequently referred to and quoted, though it is not actually in print and it is, as often as not, misunderstood, both in itself and in its context. The proper way to end this book, therefore, is to attempt to place it in its context, to explain what came before and after, as that led up to and influenced Gray, and as he affected what followed. The journal is a gem - one of the finest pieces of travel writing in English - and one of the earliest. It clearly began the cult of tourism in the Lakes but, more than that, it began a revolution in attitudes towards wild scenery.

Early Attitudes to Wild Scenery

This change in attitudes to mountains and wild scenery took place over a period of fifty years from 1720 to 1770 but it also developed into what is sometimes referred to as the Romantic revolution and, arguably, into an even wider change in intellectual, social and psychological attitudes. Such major changes in cultural climate are difficult to explain. It is usually, and not unreasonably, assumed that they are slow changes in response to social and economic changes: it is not clear what part, initiating or encouraging or merely following, individual thinkers and writers can have on those changes. If, however, we cannot be sure of the causes of the changes, we can at least describe them as they happen and then try to assess the parts played by individuals in them. In discussing the discovery of the Lake District and in trying to place Thomas Gray and his *Journal* in that process, we have additionally to remember that we are discussing its discovery by outsiders, by metropolitan intellectuals, in much the same way as the discovery of Africa in the nineteenth century might be seen to be in fact its discovery by Europeans. We have also to deal with a process with no very clearly defined beginning and an end which is arguably still unravelling. At least it is clear that at the beginning of the century mountains were usually disliked, or at least avoided, and rarely if ever praised, whereas by the end of the century the reverse was true. In the late 1720s Defoe gives the typical attitude to mountainous country when describing Westmoreland in his *Tour through the Whole Island of Great Britain* as "the wildest, most barren and frightful of any that I have passed over". It does not matter that he may not in fact have ventured north of Lancaster. Even Hampstead was too high for him: " 'tis so near heaven [he writes of the Heath], that I dare not say it can be a proper situation, for any but a race of mountaineers, whose lungs have been so used to a rarify'd air". Defoe is clearly anti-mountains *per se*, but the absence of appreciation is as eloquent as the presence of depreciation. There are no descriptive poems or travel journals or mountain landscape paintings from that earlier time.

The First Signs of Changed Attitudes

The situation began to change in the 1740s and the crucial event in that change seems to have been the Jacobite Rebellion of 1745. Not only did that nearly-successful rising focus fearful attention on the north but its defeat brought greater security, a realization of the need for better communications, and a wider interest by the southern middle classes in the remoter areas of the kingdom, greater familiarity and awareness bringing a fashionable acceptance. George Smith wrote articles for *The*

Gentleman's Magazine in 1745/6 on the siege of Carlisle and followed them with a description of a journey to Cross Fell mountain. He described this area as the British Alps, "ten months bury'd in snow", and praised it for its "romantic scenes". In November of 1747 he wrote a description of the Caldbeck Fells. Most people now find these the grassiest and roundest and least exciting of the Lake District fells but Smith claims for them "insuperable precipices and towering peaks and exhilarating landscapes of a quite different and more romantic air than any part of the general ridge". Smith's two uses of the word "romantic" are interesting in view of what followed but he appears to use the word loosely to mean "sentimentally exciting". His articles were followed by an even more interesting anonymous one in December of 1748. This describes Windermere with the recognizable vocabulary of tourist appreciation as "one of the most glorious appearances that ever struck the eye of the traveller with transport [....] mountain above mountain, forming the most stupendious [*sic*] theatre, presenting the most sublime scenes that human sight can possibly make room for". With such language the tourist age has clearly arrived. Further articles by Smith followed, clearly capitalizing upon this existing interest, on a visit to the wad mines in Borrowdale and on a storm in St John's in the Vale. Smith was followed by two other pioneers, both clerics from the Lake District hinterland rather than its heart, and then by a band of professional men, not aristocrats or men of commerce but a lawyer, an agriculturalist, an antiquarian, and an artist, who set about the business of re-discovering northern Britain, not just for a new generation but for a new mentality, preparing the way for a new era in intellectual and cultural history.

Revd John Dalton

Which of the two pioneers was the first to put pen to paper is not entirely clear but the first to appear in print was the Revd John Dalton of Dean, near Cockermouth, whose *Poem addressed to Two Ladies,* was published in a pamphlet in 1755. Dalton's poem is not a great work in itself but it is typical of a particular, sentimental point of view, viewing horror at a safe distance, which later developed into the taste for the

Picturesque. The poem, already quoted in the course of the journal entry about Borrowdale, achieved a wide currency and so must have had some influence in attracting attention to the Keswick area.

Revd Dr John Brown

The other and more original pioneer is the Revd Dr John Brown, who was brought up in Wigton, within sight of Skiddaw, and whose *Description of the Lake at Keswick* may have been written before Dalton's poem in 1752. It is probably safer, however, to date it from its first publication as a letter in the *London Chronicle* in April of 1766. It is the first major piece of prose writing to appreciate and analyse the beauty of wild scenery and it was influential upon a number of important writers as well as being widely read among a more general reading public. After comparing Keswick to Dovedale, Brown makes his most famous assertion about the major constituents of wild scenery.

> Were I to analyze the two places into their constituent principles, I should tell you, that the full perfection of KESWICK consists of three circumstances, *Beauty, Horror,* and *Immensity* united; the second of which is alone found in *Dovedale.* Of Beauty it hath little: Nature having left it almost desart: Neither its small extent nor the diminutive and lifeless form of the hills admit magnificence.... But to give you a complete idea of these three perfections, as they are joined in KESWICK, would require the united powers of *Claude, Salvator,* and *Poussin.* The first should throw his delicate sunshine over the cultivated vales, the scattered cots, the groves, the lake, and wooded islands. The second should dash out the horror of the rugged cliffs, the steeps, the hanging woods, and foaming waterfalls; while the grand pencil of *Poussin* should crown the whole with the majesty of the impending mountains.

It becomes clear that his description is written from the summit of Walla Crag but he also descends to the valley bottom and, writing with enthusiasm and eloquence, he recommends taking a walk by still moonlight.

I will carry you to the top of a cliff, where if you dare approach the ridge, a new scene of astonishment presents itself, where the valley, lake, and islands, seem lying at your feet; where this expanse of water appears diminished to a little pool amidst the vast immeasurable objects that surround it; for here the summits of more distant hills appear beyond those you had already seen; and rising behind each other in successive ranges and azure groups of craggy and broken steeps, form an immense and awful picture, which can only be expressed by the image of a tempestuous sea of mountains....Let me now conduct you down again to the valley, and conclude with one circumstance more; which is, that a walk by still moon-light (at which time the distant waterfalls are heard in all their variety of sound) among these inchanting dales, opens a scene of such delicate beauty, repose, and solemnity, as exceeds all description.

Edmund Burke

What is wanting for the new spirit which is beginning to emerge in Smith and Dalton and Brown to solidify into a new movement is a new aesthetic, a philosophical analysis of the new attitude to beauty. This was provided by Edmund Burke in his *Philosophical Enquiry into the Origin of our Ideas of the Sublime and the Beautiful*, published in 1757. Burke was a relatively young man (28) when he wrote this treatise but it is an original work and it was very influential in encouraging an almost religious concept of a beauty that went beyond form or proportion or grace to the sublime. Burke's definition of the sublime is as follows: "Whatever is fitted in any sort to excite ideas of pain, that is to say, whatever is in any sort terrible, or operates in a manner analogous to terror, is a source of the *sublime*; that is, it is productive of the strongest emotions of which the mind is capable of feeling." This elevation of fear into a positive quality, with its corresponding reduction of beauty into something small-scale, provided a powerful new aesthetic support to the new attitudes. When Brown analyses the beauty of Keswick into its constituent principles, although he does not use Burke's vocabulary, it is "Beauty, Horror, and Immensity" that he finds, a combination which is much the same as Burke's sublime.

Brown's Influence on Thomas Gray

John Brown's pamphlet was apparently sold to tourists from the Queen's Head in Keswick and it was later printed as an addendum to West's Guide in 1780. It is mentioned by later visitors such as William Hutchinson and Thomas Pennant but its most important reader was Thomas Gray and it may well have been Brown's *Description* that prompted Gray to visit the Lake District. Since Gray never mentions the *Description* or Brown, it is impossible to be sure that this line of influence was direct but there are a number of verbal indications in Gray's *Journal*, as we have seen, which suggest not only that Gray had read Brown but that he had read him closely and may even have seen a manuscript copy of Brown's original work. Gray's *Journal*, however, was not published immediately and a number of other pioneering writers actually preceded him in publication or preparation. These writers were very different in interest and outlook, both from Gray himself and from one another: Arthur Young was an agriculturalist; William Hutchinson was pre-eminently an antiquarian; Thomas Pennant, a friend and correspondent of Gray's, was an amateur scientist; and William Gilpin, a pupil in his youth of John Brown, was an artist and, perhaps we should say, an aesthetician. Their writing is the next stage in the opening up of the Lake District. They have a quaintness now, which is interesting in small doses, especially in comparison to the simplicity of Gray, and they are pervaded by an air of exploration and discovery which it is a challenge to try to recapture.

The Early Writers on the Lakes: Young, Hutchinson, Pennant, and Gilpin

Arthur Young in fact made his tour of the Lakes in 1768, before Gray but after Brown, but did not publish the results until 1770. His interest was mainly in farming matters but he did try to write in an appropriate style when he reached Keswick.

You walk from the town first down to *Cockshutt-hill*, a small rising ground, within the amphitheatre of mountains, and has been lately planted. The view of the lake from hence is very beautiful: You have a most elegant sheet of water at your feet, of the finest colour imaginable, spotted with islands, of which you see five, and are high enough to command the water around them. [...] This is the view of the floor of this noble amphitheatre; the walls are in a different stile - sublime. To the left you look first on a hilly rock, partly covered with shrubby wood, and further on, upon a chain of tremendous rocks, near 400 yards high; their feet are spread with hanging woods, but their heads bare, broken, irregular.

As description it is confused and bland but it is interesting in that it already uses the tourist vocabulary - "amphitheatre", "sublime", "tremendous" - and in showing that the tourist itinerary - to Cockshut Hill and round the lake and down to Lodore (in a later passage) - had already been established.

Hutchinson was a lawyer from Barnard Castle in County Durham: his *Excursion into the Lakes in Westmorland and Cumberland* was published in 1776. He comes across as a pleasant man, sensible, acute, a little wordy but lively in his writing. He is a useful counterpoint to Gray, giving much more detail of the travelling conditions. For instance, he is as lavish in his praise of the landlord of the White Swan at Penrith - "above his fellows in propriety of manners" - as he is scathing about his "drunken soporiferous Innkeeper" at Keswick and of the "impertinent, talkative, lying pilot" of his "nasty, leaking fishing boat" on Derwentwater. His set- piece description of his outing on Derwentwater at night is worth comparing with Gray. It is unoriginally stylized in manner and awkwardly punctuated but it shows sensitivity and enterprise.

We returned to Keswick. The romantic scenes upon the lake, induced us to take a boat at night, under the favour of the moon, which was near the full - We began our voyage soon after the moon was risen, and had illumined the top of Skiddaw, but, from the intercepting mountains, had not (within the ascent of an hour) reached the lake; we were surrounded with a solemn gloom, the stillness of the evening rendered the voice of the waterfalls tremendous, as they, in all their variety of sounds, were re-echoed from every cliff. - The summits of the rocks, when they began to receive the rising rays, appeared as if crowned with turrets of silver, from which the stars departed for their nightly round. As the gloom below grew deeper, objects around us seemed to rise to view, as surging on the first morning from chaos. The water was a plain of sable, studded over with gems reflected from the starry firmament; the groves which hung upon the feet of the mountains were wrapt in darkness; and all below was one grave and majestic circle of Skiddaw.

After this expedition, Hutchinson made a bold ascent of Skiddaw, bold in that they were beset by a bad thunderstorm on the summit and descended the hill "wet and fatigued". He describes the air at that altitude as "remarkably sharp and thin, compared with that in the valleys" and noticed that "respiration seems to be performed with a kind of asthmatic oppression". Many out of condition or ageing walkers would still confirm that observation. Hutchinson is a treat to read, though he is no poet.

Thomas Pennant is no poet either but also worth reading, if for different reasons. He is sometimes mocked for his stately seriousness but he must have been an interesting man. He was brought up by his Welsh wet nurse to speak Welsh, an unusual accomplishment in an eighteenth-century gentleman. He lost his young wife early on in his marriage and seems to have consoled himself with travel and natural history. He was a generous man, giving the profits of one of his books to a Welsh charity school, though illiberal enough (after the manner of his times) to observe with pleasure "old age, idiocy, and even infants of three years of age, contributing to their own support [at a workhouse in Whitehaven], by the pulling of oakum" [loose fibre from old rope]. He made a journey into Scotland, calling in at the Lake District on the way and publishing a book based on the journey, titled *A Tour in Scotland and Voyage to the Hebrides 1772*. He was more interested in observations of natural history and in antiquities than in wild scenery as such, but he is clearly aware of what he was supposed to feel at Keswick.

> Arrive near the *Elysium* of the North, the vale of *Keswick*, a circuit between land and water of about twenty miles. From an eminence above, command a fine bird's eye view of the broad fertile plain, the town of *Keswick*, the white church of *Crosthwaite*, the boasted lake of *Derwentwater*, and the beginning of that of *Bassenthwaite*, with a full sight of the vast circumjacent mountains that guard this delicious spot.

Gilpin is similar in earnestness and philanthropy to Pennant. He was born in Carlisle and as a young man received pre-university tuition from the John Brown whom we have already mentioned as a key figure several times. He remained friendly with Brown for a number of years and corresponded with him, though their friendship ceased in the 1750s, apparently owing to a misunderstanding about a loan. Brown may well have had a shaping influence on Gilpin's ideas about landscape and joined with him in early visits to Keswick. Gilpin wrote a book, *Observations relative chiefly to Picturesque Beauty* (1786), similar to Hutchinson's *Excursion* in that it records a journey through the Lake District, different in that there runs through it a commentary on the pictorial potential of the scenery, following picturesque principles propounded by Gilpin. Gilpin has been much derided but his ideas are sensible, even if his style is ponderous and his outlook rather limited. His description of Derwentwater is typical.

> Of all the lakes in these romantic regions, the lake we are now examining, seems to be the most generally admired. It was once admirably characterized by an ingenious person,[5] who, on his first seeing it, cryed out, "*Here is beauty indeed - Beauty lying in the lap of Horror!*" We do not often find a happier illustration. Nothing conveys an idea of *beauty* more strongly than the lake; nor of *horror*, than the

---

5. The late Mr Avison, organist of St Nicholas at Newcastle upon Tyne [Gilpin's note].

mountains; and the former *lying in the lap* of the latter, expresses in a strong manner the mode of their combination. The late Dr Brown, who was a man of taste, and had seen every part of this country, singled out the scenery of this lake for it's peculiar beauty.

Gilpin wanted to compose a picture along geometrical lines out of the scenery he saw and he recommended the transposition of walls, animals, trees and so on to balance the symmetry he was looking for. He would find fault with fine landscapes where his compositional principles were not in evidence. All that he was doing was adjusting the viewpoint to obtain a pleasing picture in much the same way as most people do now when they adjust what they see in the viewfinder of their camera. For Norman Nicholson this was a basic betrayal and he reserved for Gilpin and the Picturesque movement after him his strongest fire.

> They set up an entirely false relation between themselves and nature. For the picturesque is an appalling distortion of perception [....] In the Picturesque, the only creative act is that of man himself, a small, mean, self-satisfied manipulation of an abstract landscape. The Picturesque reduces the world to a mere scribbling pad for man; it makes a convenience of nature. It denies all dimensions to nature except one - and that a false one. It denies the intricate reality of the world, the biological, geological, organic, physical complexity of which rock, water, air, grass, tree, bird, beast, and man himself are all part. It is, in fact, not even a half-truth, or a quarter-truth, but a lie.

Fortunately, the Picturesque movement was an artistic cul-de-sac. Gilpin was, however, immensely influential for a time, both in popularizing the Lake District and in propounding a certain aesthetic attitude to it. He was modest enough to have been aware that he could not reach the levels of spirituality later reached by Wordsworth.

This group of writers prepared the way for the Romantics in that they re-discovered the Keswick-Grasmere-Ullswater area, raising metropolitan awareness, changing aesthetic and literary attitudes in the growing and more mobile middle-class. Since his *Journal* was not (as we have seen) published until 1775, Gray comes nearly at the end of this group of writers but that position is pivotal. He is linked to his predecessors by his clear debt to John Brown's *Description*, while his influence on his successors is evident both in the itinerary followed by later tourists, which was closely modelled on his route, and in the many references to his writing in later travellers and poets. Among these the chief and final debtor was Wordsworth.

Wordsworth's Debt to Gray

Wordsworth's poetry can now be seen as the destination towards which all these writers were travelling (purists will dismiss this suggestion as teleology - the view that sees events only in the light of their consequence). Wordsworth's vision of man's relationship to nature, his concept of an education through fear and love by nature, is the balancing philosophy which ultimately emerges from the pioneer breakaways from fear and disgust towards respect based on awe. In his own career Wordsworth repeats this process, starting in imitation of Gray and Brown, even in verbal detail, in *An Evening Walk*, and working towards his own vision in *The Prelude*. We tend now to see the Lake District through Wordsworth's eyes but because we also tend not to see that vision in its historical context, we see it as a more benign, less robust vision than it really is. Fear or awe is an important constituent in it and a look at the landscape through earlier eyes, especially through Gray's eyes, may challenge us all into questioning and developing our own reactions to wild scenery.

Other Contributing Factors

This account of the discovery of the Lake District has been dominated by the part played by writers but there were other factors favourable to that discovery which affected its timing and speedy progress. If the discovery began in 1745, then by 1775 it was well-established and spreading out from the intelligentsia to the middle classes. The most important physical factor acting upon this development and spread, as has been rightly observed by most commentators on this change, was the great improvement in the construction and maintenance of roads. There had been real difficulties in reaching Carlisle during the 1745 rebellion: Wade had found it impossible to get through from Newcastle in the east and Cumberland had experienced difficulties in getting across Shap. Their difficulties were, of course, greatly increased by the fact that they were trying to move large numbers of men, together with heavy equipment, in the depths of winter but that situation did bring attention to the problem. Roads began to be turnpiked in the area in the 1750s and 1760s: from Brough to Eamont Bridge in 1753, from Cockermouth to Keswick and from Keswick to Penrith in 1762. Gray mentions the condition of the roads at several points in his journal, to note the improved condition or the unfinished state. Two competing coach services between Carlisle and London were inaugurated in 1775, bringing the travelling time from the capital down to 3 days. The cost was £3.10s for an inside seat and you were allowed a mere 14lbs weight in luggage. As Macaulay later remarked, "A traveller must be freed from all apprehension of being murdered or starved before he can be charmed by the bold outlines and rich tints of the hills."

Maps also improved dramatically from 1770 onwards. Gray appears, from the spellings of place-names which he quotes, to have used a 1760s map by Thomas Kitchen, full of major mistakes and drawn to a large scale. A much more accurate map soon appeared. Thomas Donald's "New Map of the County of Cumberland on a scale of one inch to the mile" was sold by no less a person than Mr Wordsworth (presumably the poet's father) in Cockermouth for £1.11s.6d. Maps continued to improve, especially after the Ordnance Survey began surveying the counties in 1801, though it did not reach Cumberland until 1860! Landscape prints, as we have seen, also became popular and the works of Thomas Smith and William Bellers and later of Joseph Farington were influential in making north country beauty spots well-known.

New inns were built and improved their standards, advertising themselves as "now greatly enlarged and fitted up in a genteel and commodious manner". Tourist amenities, such as guided walks and boat trips with musical accompaniments or echoing guns, were provided. It was possible to hire a post-chaise at 9d per mile. An eccentric named Joseph Pocklington instituted some spectacular regattas and mock battles on Derwentwater in the 1780s. West produced his guide-book in 1768, which was enlarged by William Cockin in 1770 and re-issued constantly in new editions over the next thirty years. Curiously, *The Cumberland Pacquet* complained in 1775 that "it is a little surprising that the coal-works here [Whitehaven] have not attracted more the notice of people who travel in search of curiosities; especially when the natural grandeurs of Keswick and its neighbourhood have been so justly and admiredly celebrated by some of the most eminent in the literary world!"

One of the factors affecting the timing of the growth of interest in the Lake District was the decline of the Grand Tour from 1789 onwards. The war with France in 1757 had not noticeably affected the numbers of gentlemen taking the Grand Tour, but war with revolutionary France in the 1790s was seen to be more total and more threatening. Holidays at home began to replace holidays on the continent but the style of the Grand Tour left its mark. Part of that Tour had been the crossing of the Alps and that experience helped to develop a taste for excitement in the mountains.

Gray's Place in this Cultural Change

The extraordinary feature of this cultural change that we have been describing is the speed of its occurrence. While one can see early tendencies in its direction in the 1740s and 1750s, the major acceleration occurs in the late 1760s. While the general assumption with all such cultural changes is that they are ideological responses to social and economic changes and that individual contributions are more in the nature of symptoms than causes, it would appear in this case that we can trace the changes to individual people in particular places at definite times: to John Brown on Walla Crag on the night of the September harvest moon in 1765 and to Thomas Gray in Borrowdale on 3rd October, 1769. This is not to say that without these two writers Romanticism would not have occurred. Rather, it is to say that Brown's *Description* and Gray's *Journal* were so influential that they have to be seen as ideological catalysts of a revolutionary and transforming nature. No doubt the catalysts worked because all the other elements were ready and waiting: a receptive public, a network of fresh roads, parallel awakenings in landscape art and gardening, the emergence of a new aesthetic theory, and new interests in philanthropy, anthropology, and education. All this developed into a mental emancipation and exploration, supported by a new sensitivity to landscape, to the primitive and the natural. One of the objectives of this re-adjustment of man to his surroundings was a search for a new kind of interdependence between man and his environment, going far beyond the mere physical interdependence. And if all this connected development is true, then we have to see Gray's *Journal* as a more original and influential work than his better known *Elegy*.

This may well seem to be an extravagant claim, because we are not used to looking at Gray as a prose writer. Yet Johnson, who had little else good to say about Gray, grudgingly confessed that "He that reads his epistolary narrative wishes that to travel, and to tell his travels, had been more his employment". More enthusiastically, that great Romantic critic, William Hazlitt, declared that, "If his poetry is sometimes finical and pedantic, his prose is quite free from affectation. He pours his thoughts out upon paper as they arise in his mind without pretence or constraint, from the pure impulse of learned leisure and contemplative indolence." That kind of indolence may well be out of fashion now and it is certainly hard to find contemporary appreciation of Gray. However, one contemporary critic, William Ruddick, rightly sees Gray as "a notable precursor of the Romantic writers who were to engage in a profound exploration of the links between man and nature in the Lake District". It is the redemptive function of such an exploration, the discovery of peace and beauty in an endangered harmony, which Ruddick rightly points to as the reward of rediscovering the Lake District through the eyes of Gray.

BIBLIOGRAPHY, ACKNOWLEDGEMENTS, NOTES ON SOURCES

MOST of the material for this book was picked up piece-meal while retracing Gray's footsteps. Some books were, however, in constant use and a reader might also like to consult them.

Correspondence of Thomas Gray, edited by Paget Toynbee and Leonard Whibley, revised by H.W.Starr, in three volumes, Oxford: The Clarendon Press, 1971.

The Poems of Thomas Gray, William Collins, Oliver Goldsmith, edited by Roger Lonsdale, London: Longman, 1969

R.H. Ketton-Cremer, *Thomas Gray: A Biography*, Cambridge: Cambridge U.P., 1955.

Grevel Lindop, *A Literary Guide to the Lake District*, London: Chatto and Windus, 1993.

Robert Mack, *Thomas Gray: A Life*, London: Yale U.P., 2000.

Norman Nicholson, *The Lakers*, London: Robert Hale, 1955; re-issued in softback by Cicerone Press of Milnthorpe in 1995.

Nikolaus Pevsner, *Cumberland and Westmorland*, Buildings of England series, Harmondsworth: Penguin, 1967; also the volumes on *The West Riding* and *North Lancashire*.

I should also like to thank the following: Canon Walter Ewbank of Carlisle for his translation of Gray's Alcaic Ode; Mr and Mrs John Murray, for access to the Gray notebooks and for their generous help and interest; Jane Wallis of the Derby Museum and Art Gallery, for information about Thomas Smith of Derby; Dr Andrew White of the Lancaster City Museum, for information about Lancaster, and Dr Neil Dalziel of the Lancaster Maritime Museum, for information on the Sands crossing; Mr Stephen White, Local Studies Librarian at Carlisle Lanes Library, for constant and reliable research help.

The illustrations are from various sources. I am grateful for the copies which I have used and for permission to reproduce them. Acknowledgements are due to the following: the British Library for the maps by James Clarke; the British Museum Department of Prints for the reproduction of the painting of Lancaster Sand by J.M.W. Turner; Carlisle Public Library for the engravings by Joseph Farington, for the engraving of a View of Derwentwater by William Bellers, for the engraving of Kendal Castle by Samuel and Nathaniel Buck, and for the engraving of a View of Derwentwater by Thomas Smith; Derby Museum and Art Gallery for the engraving of Kirkstall Abbey by Thomas Smith; Lancaster City Museum for the engraving of Hornby Castle after Samuel Buck; the National Portrait Gallery for the reproduction of the portrait of Thomas Gray by Jacob Eckhardt; and the Tate Gallery for the reproduction of the painting of Gordale Scar by James Ward.

For those who wish to have chapter and verse for statements made in the introduction, commentary and conclusion, I have included the following endnotes, referenced by page-number. I have, however, deliberately tried to avoid the full weight of academic textual apparatus, while still giving appropriate supporting information.

NOTES ON SOURCES

12. For complete details of the sequence of births and deaths, see *The Parish Registers of St. Michael, Cornhill 1546-1754*, ed. by J.L. Chester, London, 1882, kept in the Guildhall Library, City of London. Dr Audley's legal opinion is given in Addendum A on pages 1195-1197 in *Gray's Correspondence*, Oxford: O.U.P., 1935.

13. I consulted two Histories of Eton College: H.C. Maxwell Lyte, *A History of Eton College 1440-1910*, London: Macmillan, 1911, and Christopher Hollis, *Eton: A History*, London: Hollis & Carter, 1960.

16. The reference is to: Jean Hagstrum, *The Sister Arts*, Chicago: University of Chicago Press, 1958, p. 287.

17. Corbyn Morris's remark is taken from page 65 of Alan Macfarlane's book *Marriage and Love in England*, Oxford: Basil Blackwell, 1986

18. The Bentley edition of Gray's *Odes* is beautifully produced and the

illustrations are attractive and at times amusing. Its full reference is: *Designs by Mr R. Bentley for Six Poems by Mr T. Gray*, London: R. Dodsley, 1753.

19. The Latin quotations come from an autograph notebook held by Pembroke College. A notebook for 1767 has been privately published under the title *Occasional Memorandums*, Stanford Dingley: Mill House Press, 1950.

20. Gray's interest in cookery and food can be gauged from his copy of Verral's cookery book (William Verral, *A Complete System of Cookery*, London, 1759) in the possession of the British Library, which is copiously annotated in the front and rear leaves:

21. "Effeminacy": this word meant "delicacy, like a woman's", but *not* "homosexuality". Temple's remark comes in an article in *The London Magazine* in 1772. Arnold's remark comes in his essay on Gray in *Essays in Criticism* (Second series), 1888, while David Cecil's remarks come in his book, *Two Quiet Lives*, London: Constable, 1989 (paperback edition).

22. The details of the biography referred to on this page are as follows: R.H. Ketton-Cremer, *Thomas Gray: A Biography*, Cambridge: C.U.P., 1955. For evidence of homosexuality, see George Rousseau in *Perilous Enlightenment*, Manchester: Manchester U.P., 1991. Rousseau claims that there is a "mountain of evidence" of Gray's homosexuality. The only evidence he gives is a quotation made by Gray from a poem by Anacreon in a letter to West. Rousseau suggests that the quotation is meant to suggest to West a clearly homosexual passage later in the poem. As the passage is 50 lines later, it is not wholly convincing.

23. Gray's distress about the prospect of his portrait appearing with his poems can be checked in the letter to Walpole written on 13th Feb., 1753: "... [I] can't bear even the Idea!"

24. The contents of Gray's library are detailed in an article, "Thomas Gray's Library", by W. Powell Jones in *Modern Philology* (35), 1938, pp. 257-78 .

25. See for example Gray's remarks to Mason on his (Mason's) wife's approaching death: "(....what could I do, were I present, more than this?), to sit by you in silence, & pity from my heart[....] May he who made us, the Master of our pleasures and of our pains, preserve and support you." (28 March, 1767)

29. The reference is to: Michael ffinch, *Portrait of the Howgills and the Upper Eden Valley*, London: Robert Hale, 1982, p. 81.
30. The reference is to: William Hutchinson, *An Excursion to the Lakes*, London: J. Wilkie, 1776, p. 27.
31. The reference is to: William Wordsworth, *The Prelude* (1805), Bk 11, ll. 279ff.
41. The reference is to: Alexander Pope, *Essay on Man*, Epistle IV, line 129.
43. The best collection of Claude glasses that I know of is in the Science Museum in London: they have about a dozen in various shapes and sizes. Dove Cottage also has a couple. Norman Nicholson's poem is titled *Thomas Gray in Patterdale* and can be found in *Selected Poems*, London: Faber, 1972 (paperback), p. 48. Nicholson's other comments come from *The Lakers* (*op. cit.*), p. 41 and p. 48.
48. I have not been able to track this remark to its original site but it is quoted in *Coleridge among the Lakes and Mountains*, selected and edited by Roger Hudson, London: The Folio Society, 1991, p.163.
50. This remark can be found in P.W. Clayden, *The Early Life of Samuel Rogers*, London: Smith Elder, 1887, p. 92: "Said Mr Gray devoted a month to the Lakes; that his cicerone, Hodgkins, who was a sensible fellow, described him as difficult to be pleased, and peevish from ill-health; that he could not ride on a horse, and would not go on water".
53. Gray's copy of Linnaeus is in the keeping of University of London Library. Pennant's description of the erne is in his *British Zoology*, Volume 1, Warrington: William Eyres, 1776, p. 149.
54. Wilberforce's tour has been reprinted and edited by his great-great grandson: *Journey to the Lake District from Cambridge*, Stocksfield: Oriel Press, 1983.
55. This line of Milton's comes from *Samson Agonistes*, l. 89.
60. This letter by Archibald Bower (an adventurer of dubious moral principles) to Charles Lyttelton is held in photostat form in the archives at Hagley House (fol. 263). Tim Clayton discusses the importance of landscape prints in *The English Print 1688-1802*, Yale University Press, 1997, p.157.
61. These adverts come from the pages of *The Cumberland Pacquet*, which commenced publication from Whitehaven in 1774 and is kept on microfilm in the Lanes Library, Carlisle.
62. For an account of Rawnsley's life see Eleanor F. Rawnsley, *Canon Rawnsley:*

An Account of his Life, Glasgow: Maclehose, Jackson, 1923. For full accounts of aesthetic categories, see Christopher Hussey, *The Picturesque,* London: G.P. Putnam, 1927 (still an excellent book), and Malcolm Andrews, *The Search for the Picturesque,* Stanford: Stanford U.P., 1989.

68. Camden's *Britannia* was first published in Latin in 1587. This would have posed no problems to Gray but there were a number of 18th century reprints. For Keats's visit, see Caroline Kyros Walker's attractive book: *Walking North with Keats,* New Haven & London: Yale U.P., p. 156.

72. Grevel Lindop, in his attractive book, *A Literary Guide to the Lake District,* supposes that Gray called at the Castle Inn ("Gray would not recognise it now", p. 152). But that inn did not exist then, whereas there was one at Ouse Bridge itself.

82. The reference is to Edward Young's *Night Thoughts,* 1.55 & 1.393. I consulted an edition with illustrations by William Blake, published in New York: Dover Publications, 1975, p. 3 and p. 14.

83. William Hudson's *Flora Anglica* is held in the Local History section of the Lanes Library in Carlisle. *A Flora of Cumbria,* edited by Geoffrey Halliday, was published by the Centre for North-West Regional Studies at Lancaster University in 1997.

84. I am grateful for information on charr to the Angling Correspondent of *The Cumberland and Westmorland Herald* of Penrith. For the suggestion that the opposition between Picturesque nature and unpicturesque industry comes later with Gilpin, see Stephen Copley's interesting essay, "William Gilpin and the Black Lead Mine" in *The Politics of the Picturesque,* Cambridge: Cambridge U.P., 1994, p. 49. For more information on the mine, see Ian Tyler, *Seathwaite Wad,* Carlisle: Blue Rock Publications, 1995.

89. Wordsworth's *The Waggoner* was composed in 1805, dedicated to Charles Lamb, and first published in 1819.

90. "She saw that there had been bad habits; that Sunday travelling had been a common thing...." These words are spoken of Mr Elliot in *Persuasion,* Oxford: O.U.P. (Oxford Illustrated edition), p.161.

91. The reference is to William Gilpin, *Observations relative chiefly to Picturesque Beauty,* London: R. Blamire, 1786 (facsimile ed., Richmond, 1973), p. 166.

92. William Empson complained that, "Many people, without being

communists, have been irritated by the complacence in the massive calm of the poem". See: *Some Versions of Pastoral*, London: Hogarth Press, 1986, p. 5.

93. These comments about James Ward are to be found on page 81 of Geoffrey Grigson's *Britain Observed*, London: Phaidon, 1975.

97. For the history of Kendal Church, see Roger Bingham, *Kendal: A Social History*, Milnthorpe: Cicerone Press, 1995, pp. 64-9.

104. Arthur Young makes this remark on p. 196 of *A Six Month's Tour through the North of England*, London: W. Strahan, 1770. Dickens's comments are from: *The Lazy Tour of Two Idle Apprentices*, contained in *Christmas Stories* (Oxford Illustrated Dickens), London: O.U.P., 1956, pp. 721, 2.

110. See *The Parish Registers of the Parish Church of Cartmel*, published by the Lancashire Parish Register Society; and T. Pape, *The Sands of Morecambe Bay*, Morecambe, 1947, who states (p.16) that the Cartmel parish registers from the late sixteenth century to 1880 contain records of 141 deaths by drowning on the Sands.

117. David Hill's beautifully illustrated *In Turner's Footsteps*, London: John Murray, 1993 (paperback) is worth consulting for Gray's influence on Turner.

122. For information on John Ray, see C.E. Raven, *John Ray, Naturalist: His Life and Works*, Cambridge: CUP, 1942. Margaret Drabble's remarks come in her book: *A Writer's Britain*, London: Thames and Hudson, 1979, pp. 125ff.

125. See Geoffrey Grigson, *op. cit.*, p. 81.

133. See Thomas West: *A Guide to the Lakes in Cumberland, Westmorland and Lancashire, 1784 (3rd edition)*, facsimile edition by Woodstock Books, 1989.

134. For Defoe's remark about Westmoreland, see *Tour through the whole Island of Great Britain*, Harmondsworth: Penguin Classics, 1986, p. 550; the remark about Hampstead is on p. 339.

135. The full title of Dalton's poem, which is printed as an Addendum to West's Guide (2nd edition onwards) and was originally printed as a pamphlet in London by Rivington and Dodsley in 1755, is: *A Descriptive Poem addressed to Two Ladies*.

136. For more information on Brown see my book on his life and works: William Roberts, *A Dawn of Imaginative Feeling*, Carlisle: Northern Academic

Press, 1995.

137. Burke's essay has been reprinted in an edited edition: Edmund Burke, *A Philosophical Enquiry into the Origin of our Ideas of the Sublime and Beautiful*, ed. by J.T. Boulton, London: Routledge, 1958.

139-141. The full details of the works referred to in these pages are as follows: Arthur Young, *A Six Months Tour through the North of England*, London: W. Strahan, 1770; William Hutchinson, *An Excursion to the Lakes*, London: J. Wilkie, 1776; Thomas Pennant, *A Tour in Scotland and Voyage to the Hebrides 1772*, Edinburgh: Birlinn, 1998 (modern reprint); William Gilpin, *Observations chiefly relative to Picturesque Beauty*, London: R. Blamire, 1786.

143. The verbal detail in *An Evening Walk* which echoes Brown and Gray is in the lines near the end of that poem (ll. 433 & 445) describing "The song of mountain streams unheard by day / Now hardly heard" and "The distant forge's swinging thump profound".

144. I culled this quotation from Peter Bicknell's article in the catalogue accompanying an exhibition in the Fitzwilliam Museum, entitled *Beauty, Horror and Immensity*, Cambridge: C.U.P., 1981, p. xii.

145. A good account of contemporary maps is given by John Higham, *The Antique County Maps of Cumberland*, Carlisle: Bookcase, 1997.

146. See Johnson's "Life of Gray" in *Lives of the Poets*, London: Dent (Everyman), 1975, p. 464. Hazlitt's remarks come in *Lectures on the English Poets*, London: Dent (Everyman), 1910, p. 118.

147. William Ruddick's remarks come in the only attempt that has been made to assess Gray's travel writing in an essay in *Thomas Gray: Contemporary Essays*, Liverpool: Liverpool U.P., 1993.

EPILOGUE

Alcaic Ode

In the Book at the Grande Chartreuse among the Mountains of Dauphiné

O Tu, severi religio loci
Quocumque gaudes nomine (non leve
    Nativa nam certa fluenta
        Numen habet, veteresque silvas;

Praesentiorem et conspicimus Deum
Per invias rupes, fera per iuga,
    Clivosque praeruptos, sonantes
        Inter aquas, nemorumque noctem;

Quam si repostus sub trabe citrea
Fulgeret auro, et Phidiaca manu)
    Salve vocanti rite, fesso et
        Da placidam iuveni quietem.

Quod si invidendis sedibus, et frui
Fortuna sacra lege silentii
    Vetat volontem, me resorbens
        In medios violenta fluctus:

Saltem remoto des, Pater, angulo
Horas senectae ducere liberas;
    Tutumque vulgari tumultu
        Surripias, hominumque curis.

Gray's Alcaic Ode Translated

Some godhead haunts this harsh and holy place
(His name, who knows? No petty god, for sure).
    Its own perennial waters grace
    An abbey, its ancient woods immure.

Among the trackless crags, steep mountain-sides,
Grim peaks, by sounding torrents, forest-gloom,
    More truly, know, a god resides,
    Than should some Phidian statue loom,

Glowing in gold and marble, under roof
Of fragrant timbers. Greetings, O good Lord,
    That hauntest this wild place aloof,
    And if in prayer I strike a chord

Acceptable, then let me find my peace,
Young and yet weary, here. If jealous Fate
    Withholds for now my longed release
    And thrusts me back to things I hate,

To crowds and noise; then grant me in full age
That I may win some corner, far from strife,
    And there, as in an hermitage,
    Contentedly conclude my life.

W.F.E.

156 *Thomas Gray's Journal*

INDEX (1) PLACES